Microsoft

FIRST GENERATION

Microsoft
FIRST GENERATION

THE SUCCESS SECRETS OF THE VISIONARIES WHO LAUNCHED A TECHNOLOGY EMPIRE

CHERYL D. TSANG

John Wiley & Sons, Inc.

New York · Chichester · Weinheim · Brisbane · Singapore · Toronto

Published by John Wiley & Sons, Inc.
Published simultaneously in Canada.

This publication is designed to provide accurate and authoritative information in regard to the subject matter covered. It is sold with the understanding that the publisher is not engaged in rendering professional services. If legal, accounting, medical, psychological or any other expert assistance is required, the services of a competent professional person should be sought.

Library of Congress Cataloging-in-Publication Data:
Tsang, Cheryl D., 1947–
    Microsoft first generation : the success secrets of the
visionaries who launched a technology empire / Cheryl D. Tsang.
        p.   cm.
    Includes index.
    ISBN 0-471-33206-2 (cloth)
    1. Microsoft Corporation—History. 2. Businessmen—United States—Biography. 3. Computer software industry—United States—History.
I. Title. II. Title: Microsoft 1st generation.
HD9696.63.U64M538   1999
338.7′610053′0973—dc21   99-27007
                                                                    CIP

Printed in the United States of America.

10 9 8 7 6 5 4 3 2 1

For my family: Rick Tsang, Joshua Tsang,
and Erin Chastain Matayoshi

CONTENTS

Acknowledgments   *ix*
Introduction   *xi*

1   Bob O'Rear: 1
     "The Mathematician," 1977–1993

2   Scott Oki: 23
     "The Force," 1982–1992

3   Richard Brodie: 47
     "The Dilettante," 1981–1994

4   Russell Borland: 69
     "The Author," 1980–1997

5   Neil Evans: 87
     "The Professor," 1983–1994

6   Dave Neir: 113
     "The CPA," 1983–1993

7   Ida Cole: 131
     "The Independent," 1984–1990

 8 Min Yee: 149
    "Min," 1985–1992

 9 Ron Harding: 179
    "The Techie," 1986–1990

10 Paul Sribhibhadh: 195
    "The Diplomat," 1987–1997

11 Russell Steele: 213
    "The Musician," 1986–1994

12 Trish Millines Dziko: 227
    "The Athlete," 1988–1996

Afterword   243
Index   249

ACKNOWLEDGMENTS

This book belongs to the 12 men and women who trusted me to accurately share their stories. I hope I have been equal to their trust. In a timely and efficient manner they gave me everything I asked for: information, corrections, answers to questions, and follow-up interviews. I am truly in their debt.

A special thanks goes to Scott Oki for his unwavering patience and support for this project and for opening the door.

Min Yee was incredibly helpful and supportive, and for that I am grateful.

My husband, Rick Tsang, a 13-year veteran of Microsoft, acted as my agent and taught me the business side of publishing a book. Thank you for your support, Rick.

I am fortunate to have a truly fine editor at John Wiley & Sons, Henning Gutmann. Thanks, Henning, for believing in the project and for steering it in the right direction.

Thanks also to my developmental editor, Jon Beckmann, who understood the nature of the project and was a pleasure to work with.

The following people deserve a big thanks: Lisa Davisson, John Pinette, April Hill, David Jaworski, Patty Stonesifer, Bonnie Tabb, and Paul Shoemaker.

Thanks to Elton Welke, former publisher at Microsoft Press and now board chairman of Elton-Wolfe Publishing for his take on the original manuscript. In addition, I'd like to thank Chris Banks for getting the ball rolling.

For providing places of refuge and solace, I'd like to thank my mother, Dolores Loganbill, my sister, Christine Riggs, and my friends, Debby Shearer and Wendy Lee Kanno. A great big thanks and a kiss to my grandson, Hunter Matayoshi, for keeping me in touch with pure joy and whimsy when I needed it the most.

Many thanks to my comrades-in-writing, Sheri (Sherrell) Short, Billee Escott, and Frances Sonneband for being tough critics, for believing in me, and for pushing me.

I owe a big thanks to Mick and Penny Deal for the use of their fabulous library on such short notice.

My son, Joshua Tsang, became my technical as well as moral support person. Thanks, son.

Many thanks to my daughter, Erin Chastain Matayoshi, for her assistance and encouragement.

Thanks also to David Moss, Jamie Hass, Bruce Milne, Joyce Yoshikawa, Damian Cordova, Harold Taniguchi, Fran Shultz, Ryo Matayoshi, Elisa Del Rosario, Annette Freeman, Jeremy Jaech, Tom Alberg, and Jeff Tarter.

Finally, I'd like to thank all the folks at John Wiley & Sons for their professionalism, in particular, Jeffrey Brown for his initial interest.

INTRODUCTION:

The Secrets of Success

Microsoft has been the focus of sustained and intense—nearly voyeuristic—public interest for more than a decade. However, any understanding of the company's position and influence in the electronic world needs to take into account that there were two phases in the making of Microsoft. The year 1990 is generally agreed on as the dividing point. The years prior to 1990 were spent in making and creating the company. The following years were devoted to sustaining and growing the company. In its first phase, Microsoft grew from a start-up partnership between Bill Gates and Paul Allen in 1975 to a company that dominated the software industry. This book looks at the first generation of men and women who, in the 1980s or earlier, plugged into Bill Gates's vision of the future and helped launch a technology empire that changed the Information Age.

In this book you will meet 12 of these people, from Bob O'Rear, employee number seven, who joined Microsoft in 1977, two years after its inception, and brought up MS-DOS on the first IBM PC, to Trish Millines, who began as a contract employee in 1988. How did they succeed at Microsoft? What success traits did they bring to the company? What are they doing now? My theory was that each of these men and women would succeed no matter what their endeavor. They did not prove me wrong. In following their journeys from their early lives to retirement, their success traits, often shared with their colleagues, shone through. Their individual stories are truly inspirational.

As Microsoft evolved, Bill Gates and Paul Allen hired people who were cut from their own cloth. Hiring carefully was extremely important, and they considered only brilliant and enthusiastic people—many joined fresh out of the best colleges and universities in the country and others came from the rapidly evolving computer industry. Bob O'Rear, a brilliant mathematician and programmer hired in 1977, says, "Bill and Paul led by example." They worked extraordinarily long hours, exuded passion and a drive for excellence, and pushed themselves with energy fueled by their desire to succeed. It was Scott Oki, senior VP, who coined the term *maniacal work ethic.* All were on a mission to make Microsoft the most successful company of its time. Ida Cole, the first female VP, says, "We truly believed."

Bob O'Rear recalls, "Bill and Paul were so brilliant and incisive. For such young men they had a very broad understanding of computing. They were definitely entrepreneurs. We all worked very hard. I was behind on my projects the day I walked in!"

In 1979, with 25 employees, several new computer language products, and yearly sales of $2.5 million, Bill Gates and Paul Allen made the decision to move from Albuquerque back to their native Seattle. One year later they acquired the license to the UNIX operating system and developed XENIX, an operating system for microcomputers. Microsoft was branching out.

In 1980, when IBM asked Microsoft to develop DOS for its first IBM PC, no one had any inkling that this partnership would be a turning point of Microsoft's success in the world of high technology. Soon Microsoft's operating system would be the industry standard.

The company continued to expand. In 1980, Bill hired an old college friend, Steve Ballmer, as his assistant. Steve was brilliant and savvy in his own right. His boundless enthusiasm and cheerleading style would take Microsoft to new heights of success. That same year, Russell Borland, a Ph.D., was looking for work. He saw an ad for a technical writer. "I had never heard of Microsoft. Nobody I knew had ever heard of Microsoft." Russell took the job thinking it might end in six months. But he would stay on for 17 years, almost as long as Bill Gates and Steve Ballmer. He familiarized the world with Microsoft products by writing 17 best-sellers about them. The company at that time had grown to 40 employees and annual sales of $8 million.

Microsoft was growing and changing rapidly. As the company branched out into applications, it needed someone to write them. The now legendary programmer, Charles Simonyi, came over from Xerox PARC in 1981 and very quickly talked Bill into hiring a young programmer, Richard Brodie, also from PARC, for one summer. Soon Richard was working long hours and immersed himself in writing the first version of Microsoft Word.

The year 1981 was another turning point for Microsoft. The company was reorganized as a privately held corporation. Employees could now buy shares of stock. It was the same fateful year the IBM PC was announced and Microsoft published its first version of MS-DOS.

When Scott Oki was hired in 1982, Microsoft had been concentrating on domestic sales. Scott says, "International was being sorely neglected." Scott presented Bill

Gates with a formal business plan, which simply amazed Bill. At the time, there was very little formal structure to Microsoft. Most communications were done verbally. "I didn't know anything about the international marketplace when I began, but I'm not afraid of hard work. I just thought I'd figure it out." Scott traveled constantly to establish Microsoft International. "I made some bold promises to Bill, but I delivered."

At headquarters, Microsoft was desperately in need of a business structure. Neil Evans, who left the highly successful Digital Equipment Corporation to join Microsoft, remembers that at the time the company name had no name recognition for him. Of his interviews with Steve Ballmer he says, "Steve was trying to find out about my ability to be passionate, to be dedicated, and to become really good at something." Neil, hired as chief information officer, found the company accounting system as well as the computer room in a state of chaos. He spent an exhausting year correcting the situation. "All of a sudden I was the data center guy, the hardware guy, and the business interface guy. I didn't know how to do all of those things. I had to figure it out. But I liked jumping in."

Dave Neir, a CPA, joined the same day as Neil. He didn't know anything about the company. He didn't want to commute, and he found Microsoft in the local Yellow Pages. It was close to home. Like Neil, he was leaving a large and successful company for one with less than 400 employees. He found the casual attire at Microsoft disconcerting. "I wore a three-piece suit to work for years. I did not feel comfortable in jeans and a T-shirt or Bermuda shorts." When he joined he was given stock options. "I had no idea what this company could really do. I actually thought the options were worthless."

In August 1983, Microsoft hired Jon Shirley as president. Like Neil Evans, he was shocked by the company's accounting systems. There were no sound procedures to manage a rapidly growing $50-million-a-year company. He quickly established organization and procedures within the company. He was extremely good at delegating. At an annual meeting he described the ideal Microsoft employee as the type of person "who makes things happen." It was also the year that Microsoft introduced Windows, its graphical user interface for DOS.

At the time, Microsoft was thought of as primarily a white male programmers' company. In 1984, the company hired its first female vice president, Ida Cole. Ida had had a rewarding and successful career at Apple. "I wasn't serious about Microsoft. But they were serious!" Newly divorced, Ida decided it was time to make a fresh start. "The interviews were just grueling. They went on for days." As the VP of applications, she reported to Jon Shirley and Bill Gates. She describes Microsoft as a "raw environment." "The common courtesies that were prevalent in any other professional environment were not present there. Everyone was so young and competitive." But she adds, "It was the best-run company I had ever worked for."

That year, Bill Gates appeared on the cover of *Time*. The world was beginning to take note of Microsoft. It was the first software company to generate more than $100 million in annual sales.

Although Microsoft was extremely successful in applications, computer languages, and operating systems, Bill Gates was intrigued by the newly emerging CD-ROM technology. When he hired maverick news reporter and author Min Yee in 1985 to run Microsoft Press, they spent hours discussing the new technologies. Soon Min was not only publishing books but also working on the first version of what would become Encarta, Microsoft's multimedia CD-ROM encyclopedia, which went on to sell millions of copies. Min observes, "People forget, after something has been so successful, just how uncertain its fate was in the early days."

In 1986, having grown to 1,200 employees and sales of $197 million, Microsoft became a publicly traded company, and Bill Gates became the world's youngest billionaire. Employees had no way of knowing how their lives would change as a result of their stock options. In less than five years many of them became exceedingly rich. On one hand, in addition to the other amenities offered by Microsoft, the stock options, referred to as "the Golden Handcuffs," garnered great loyalty to the company. Employees often stayed just to add to their stock options. On the other hand, Microsoft had also gained the nickname of "the Velvet Sweatshop," and the pressure to succeed often weeded out underachievers within 18 months.

By 1990, Microsoft's rise to the top and phenomenal growth caused the inevitable sign of success: bureaucracy. Ida Cole says, "A new element came to Microsoft and brought with it more bureaucracy and red tape. It was difficult to get things done." That same year, Ida Cole left the company, as did Jon Shirley. One by one Microsoft's first generation began to think about retirement. Because of their stock in the company they were financially independent and could pursue their dreams. Dave Neir says, "I always said that one year at Microsoft was like ten years at any other company. You could learn so much in a short period of time. You could make decisions and get immediate feedback on how well you did or didn't do. Scott Oki and I would go out, grab a burger, talk, and get things done." But by the early 1990s, Dave says, "I started hitting bureaucratic roadblocks. It wasn't fun anymore." One by one, the entrepreneurial generation retired.

Yet all 12 people profiled in this book agreed that their Microsoft experience was an exceptionally rewarding time in their lives. Most of them arrived at the company before the stock options had any value. They left Microsoft with feelings of nostalgia. They are a cross representation of the various organizations within Microsoft, from senior VPs to programmers to project managers. The one unifying factor for this first generation was their commitment to the company and to doing their personal best. Scott Oki says, "I was determined to succeed." Without hesitation, all 12 recalled their Microsoft experience as the ultimate career and, given the same circumstances, wouldn't hesitate to do it all over again.

At this writing, in April 1999, Microsoft is worth $450 billion. It has surpassed two giants, General Electric and IBM (companies with similar markets that were blue-chip stalwarts on the stock exchange long before Microsoft was a twinkle in the eyes of Bill Gates and Paul Allen), to become the largest and most powerful high-tech company in the world—so powerful in fact that the Department of Justice felt compelled to probe the company's competitive practices, alleged to be unfair and monopolistic. What vaulted it into such a dominant position? These 12 stories provide insights into what might be called the Microsoft Success Story.

BOB O'REAR

"The Mathematician"

Microsoft: 1977–1993

Company Mathematician

Programmer, First IBM PC

Director, Intercontinental

Bob O'Rear

"The Mathematician"

Bob O'Rear, a polite Texan with a delightful sense of humor, is not your stereotypical Microsoft executive.

His ruddy complexion and bright eyes reflect his lifelong dedication to physical exercise. In fact, Bob had planned on becoming a physical education teacher. But his college education introduced him to the world of math, and his aptitude for the discipline led to a job with the U.S. government, specializing in spy satellite technology, and then with NASA.

Bob joined Microsoft in 1977. He was employee number seven and became the company mathematician. He was the chief programmer in charge of putting MS-DOS on the first prototype IBM PC in 1980, a daunting task. At other times, he held various directors' posts—in the international division and in the sales and licensing areas.

The Path to Microsoft

Bob O'Rear was born in Wellington, Texas, a rural town of 3,500 people in the Texas Panhandle. His mother died when he was nine months old, and Bob was raised by his grandparents, who for many years were sharecroppers on a cotton farm. Bob's grandmother would tie a cottonsack around her waist and pull Bob around while she picked. He recalls, "My grandfather split the meager profits with the owner. We were a very poor family. That's the environment I grew up in."

When he graduated from high school, Bob considered his options: "The people in my hometown who had the best jobs were the one doctor, the teachers in the high school, the one lawyer, and a dentist. They were the only professional people I ever saw while I was growing up." Bob decided to become a physical education teacher. He borrowed the money from a college fund in his hometown, established for disadvantaged students, and from his uncle. Bob chuckles when he says, "I paid it all back when I went to work for Microsoft."

At the University of Texas at El Paso, Bob studied physical education. He says, "My plan was to come back and coach tennis in high school and maybe teach a science class. But I was thrown into a dormitory where 80 percent of the guys were engineers. And I was a PE major. They made fun of my major all the time. To be quite honest, the only reason I majored in PE was that I was afraid I couldn't make it in some other field." Meanwhile, his roommates griped about their calculus studies and ribbed Bob about how easy he had it as a PE major. Midway into his second year, Bob had had enough of their teasing. He signed up for a calculus course and aced it. Bob says, "I absolutely loved it! So I became a math major." After Bob received his undergraduate degree, he went on to graduate school to study math and astrophysics.

In 1966, TRW in Redondo Beach, California, hired Bob. He worked on Air Force spy satellite programs. He says,

"In those days it was quite secret that 'spy' satellites even existed, so I had to have a special government clearance." Bob helped write the programs that determined which photographs were taken and how. This was the height of the Cold War, and the United States and Russia were aiming ICBMs at each other. In addition to the spy satellite work, Bob wrote programs that optimized the trajectory of Minuteman missiles should they ever be fired at the Soviet Union.

Bob went to work for NASA in the late 1960s. "I was in Houston at Mission Control when we landed on the moon," Bob notes. He helped write the program that determined the trajectory of the command module as it reentered the earth's atmosphere. Then, in the mid-1970s, Bob and a friend from his days at TRW started a company called Texametrics. The company made automated machinery for the manufacturing extrusion business for polyurethane bottle caps, and Bob was the genius behind its software programs, which analyzed the patterns of correctly manufactured caps and caused incorrectly manufactured parts to be ejected. At Texametrics Bob learned how to work on and repair hardware, an experience that helped when he later joined Microsoft and brought up MS-DOS for the IBM PC project. But by late 1976, Bob's company was no longer doing software programs, and he felt it was time to look for other opportunities. An old friend told him about a company called Microsoft, which then was located in Albuquerque, New Mexico. Bob recalls, "They were a small company doing computer languages on microcomputers. That fit well with what I was interested in."

In 1977, Bob went to New Mexico for an interview. Laughing, he remembers, "My friend sort of prepped me as to how young Bill Gates and Paul Allen were. He said Bill looked like he was about thirteen, and I think he was actually about nineteen. It was a really small company; they only had about five employees, Bill Gates, Paul Allen, Bob Greenberg, Marc McDonald, and Steve Wood. And there was another guy named Vince; I can't remember his last name. He only stayed for about six months. I was ten years older than anybody else was." Bill and Paul interviewed Bob while they ate at a pizza parlor. "They weren't seasoned interviewers," says Bob. "There weren't a lot of pleasantries like, 'Hello. How's the weather?' But they were not rude. It was more like, 'How ya doin'? Do you know anything about the Intel 8080 processor?'

"Ten minutes into my interview with Bill, I could understand why he's done so well. He's so brilliant and perceptive and incisive. And Paul, too." Bob had just finished writing an operating system for a small machine that ran on a DECLSI-11, a computer that he had worked on at Texametrics. He discussed it with Bill and Paul. "Immediately they picked up on the salient points of that operating system without very much prompting. For such young men, they had a very broad understanding of computing." Although Bill and Paul were young and knowledgeable, they did not strike Bob as cocky: "They were definitely entrepreneurs. I thought they were, if anything, overly respectful. Maybe it was because I was quite a bit older than they were. Bill has always been very respectful of people he considers his elders. The brash parts of Bill wouldn't come out until he knew you well. But if he saw you as an enemy, then I'm sure he'd attack."

Bob was very excited about the opportunity to work at Microsoft. It was his first chance to work with computer languages, which he always wanted to do. But he was considering two other job offers: one from the University of Wyoming and one from Martin Marietta. He says, "I wasn't really looking for security. I was just looking for fun while I did my day-to-day work. Microsoft looked far better than either of the other places in that regard."

At the time, Microsoft was a very small company of young and enthusiastic people using microcomputers and working with assembly language programming. Bob recalls, "Microsoft had all the right elements. Albuquerque was a wonderful place to live. I loved it! I went to Microsoft because I thought we could *make* a few things happen. I could have gone to the University of Wyoming and *recorded* what happened or gone to Martin Marietta and *wondered* what could have happened. They were still into mainframes, not microcomputers." As a business-man, Bob felt he should look at his other offers, but right from the start, Microsoft captured his interest. He believed Microsoft had the most promising future and would best utilize his talents.

Life at Microsoft

Bob went to work for Microsoft as the company's mathe-matician. He learned how programs were put together and reworked some of the mathematics. In that first year, Bob and others developed a simulator for the 8086 chip—a 16-bit microprocessor from Intel that eventually be-came the core of the original IBM PC. It was the next chip that would come from Intel, and because it had not yet been perfected, Intel gave them the specs so that they could simulate what it would do on a big DEC machine like the one he had worked on at Texametrics. Bob moved BASIC from the 8080 microprocessor to the 8086 chip and improved it. "I did new algorithms for the transcen-dental and floating-point operations," Bob says. "We wrote 8086 BASIC so that when the 8086 chip became available there would be a language that would use it. BASIC and FORTRAN meant everything to Microsoft. They were the business at that time." Bob's work on BASIC and FORTRAN brought much more power to the languages and made the creation of software using them more desirable.

Microsoft made several products for Intel that year and found that company to be a very demanding customer. Bob recalls, "Our biggest problem was that we had to simulate the 8086 chip on a DEC 10. We had the specs on it from Intel. The chips weren't even out yet, but we were already working on BASIC that would run on the new chip. That was kind of the mode we worked in at Microsoft. That new chip became the architecture of the IBM PC, so it was really nice that we got that early start. We didn't actually have the computer to run our software on—we had to *pretend* that we had the computer and make a DEC 10 behave like it. We made a couple of errors in the way we *thought* the 8086 would work." But after six months, BASIC was ready. In the spring of 1979, Bob had his simulated 8086 BASIC up and running. He had created the program without having the computer. Bob developed the language from start to finish without actually seeing the chip.

The arithmetic in BASIC and FORTRAN had to have some backup routines to accomplish appointed tasks. These were arithmetical, the decimal and floating-point routines. "You use these arithmetic operations in the languages to model and solve engineering calculations, like stress on a concrete bridge, or business problems, like cash flow or inventory costs. I did those operations," Bob explains. "I like being at the heart of things, and I was doing the really hard-core mathematics so that applications authors could take advantage of them." The mathematical formulas embedded by Bob in the programming languages made it easier and provided more options for the designers of specific applications.

In the summer of 1978, Paul Allen and Bob spent a month bringing up BASIC on RMX80, the real-time operating system for Intel. It was a singular accomplishment by two persons—"just us and the bits," Bob remembers— and under less than ideal working conditions. It was summer in Albuquerque, and they worked in the office on weekends, when the air-conditioning was turned off. Bob shakes his head at the memory. "We were both in our Bermuda shorts and we were sweating, trying to get this RMX80 up. We had such poor documentation for the thing—it was like throwing darts in the dark trying to make our software work, but we did!"

In the late 1970s, the turf wars in the industry had not yet begun. There was a certain sharing of information. "We were desperate to have problems solved," Bob says. "There was more than enough turf for anybody to work on. As language authors, we really wanted operating systems developed so that we didn't have to do adaptations of our languages for each computer." In fact, Microsoft wanted Intel to solve more problems such as speed, memory, floating-point arithmetic, and decimal arithmetic with hardware. As the industry continued its lightning-fast growth, competition became fierce. Bob saw the change in about the mid-1980s. He says, "People are really protecting their turf now! There was no need to then. It was like leaving your house in the 1950s—you didn't have to lock your door."

Bob reminisces about the fabled Microsoft work ethic. In his first year at the company, Bob worked hard, but "not as hard as we did in subsequent years. We had more business than we could tend to." Customers wanted Microsoft to adapt computer languages to the customers' own computers and to expand and improve those languages. Laughing, Bob recalls, "We were *always* behind. I was behind on my projects the day I walked in."

Everyone except Bob liked to come to work at 10 or 11 A.M. and work until midnight or longer. Bob says, "I didn't particularly like those hours. I was kind of an early-morning person." Bob would come in at 3 or 4 A.M. and leave about 2 P.M. Bob laughs and says, "Sometimes I'd get there before these guys had even left. When they did leave it was beautiful because I could work through the day and there was no one around to disturb me."

Work went well, and Bob thrived in this environment of dedication. Bill Gates and Paul Allen taught by example. Bob says, "They were working really hard—lots of long and odd hours. There was camaraderie when working on the projects. The enthusiasm always showed up."

Bob remembers a funny story about their social life. One day Bob Greenberg, another employee, invited them all to a Saturday night party. Bob says, "I thought that sounded like a lot of fun. We'd all been working very hard. We arrived at this party and we noticed a circle of chairs in the room. Bob Greenberg told us to have a seat. This other guy shows up and we didn't know him. He said, 'Let's just go around and the first person say his name and the person next to him say the person's name who preceded him, plus their name.' It took about five minutes into this 'game' before we realized we were at a Tupperware party!" Bob stops to laugh at the memory. "Bill looked at me, I looked at him, and we both had these funny expressions on our faces. Bob was always a bit tight with a dollar. He got a free Tupperware gift for hosting the party. So here we are, all of these technology guys sitting there looking at and examining Tupperware! Bill was about nineteen or twenty and he was looking at this stuff. I actually bought some things and I still have them!"

Bob has some vivid memories of those early years and of the founder. He remembers Bill Gates traveling around the world. "Bill would go talk to companies by himself. He'd talk to Texas Instruments, Xerox, Siemens in Germany, and Machines Bull in France. They'd have a whole cadre of technical, legal, business, and marketing guys drilling him with various questions. He'd have to field all those questions or do negotiations when he'd host a Microsoft booth by himself at trade shows. He had the guts to host a booth in Paris by himself. He was dealing with people who didn't know much English. He was a one-man band. There was no one to send out with him." Bill worked around the clock to sell his products. "Sometimes he'd be on trips and he'd come back and work and do one of those twenty-four-hour stints. He'd be sleeping in his office beneath his desk or something. You just sort of ignored it and went on and did your own thing."

Microsoft did business in the early years with Apple, Tandy Radio Shack, Rockwell International, Commodore, and Wang. "The urgency in this business was pretty obvious. There were five or six programmers writing programs. If you don't have programs to sell, there's no company. Getting these programs done and sold and revenue coming in was everything. You had to move forward and keep up with the fast pace of the industry and the hardware innovation that was going on," Bob explains. There were always new disk drives that had to be taken advantage of and new microprocessors that needed languages and operating systems. At that time, Microsoft wrote computer languages and Digital Research did most of the operating systems.

Bob explains why he thought Bill and Paul's strategy was so brilliant back then. "Before Microsoft, Intel, and microprocessors, there were hardware companies creating computers, and they, or someone else, brought in a lot of programmers to write languages, programs, operating systems, and applications for *that* computer. It took a lot of work in all those areas. So they'd solve a problem. But could you move that solution anywhere else? No. All those computers were different. But with the microprocessor, you can use an Intel 8080 chip at the core; then you are able to write languages and applications that can run on many different computers. Bill and Paul understood that—that was their brilliance."

In those days, computer science majors at the University of Washington laughed at Bill Gates's faith in and vision of the future of microcomputers. Bob recalls the feelings within the industry. "I remember a lot of my friends thought that microcomputers were never going to amount to anything. Mainframes were it. I had friends who worked for IBM and UNIVAC and they thought there'd never be enough power to solve a problem with a microcomputer. But when you worked in the microcomputer environment, each year you'd see a doubling or quadrupling of the power of these computers."

In just a few years, the whole industry model began to change. Microprocessors could be installed in many different types of computers. One program could run on each of them. Bob explains why this had such an impact on the industry. "You could base your business more on volume sales than you could in the past. These huge mainframe companies had the mentality that to keep your programs running you had to have great applications on your own piece of software. There was a change in philosophy and economics those companies ignored."

In December 1978, Microsoft made a significant change. The company decided to relocate to Bellevue, Washington. Bob says, "I was very reluctant to leave Albuquerque. I'm not sure why Bill and Paul decided to move. The decision went through this long, agonizing process. Paul really wanted to be back in the Seattle area. He really missed the scenery and his family. Bill was rarely around. As long as there was an airport, he'd be in good shape."

By January 1979, Microsoft headquarters had moved to Bellevue, Washington. Shortly thereafter, the company made a brief foray into databases. Believing it could make a database work on a microcomputer, Microsoft licensed one called Microseed. Not everything the company did turned to gold, however. Microseed was a complete failure. Bob smiles and says, "I worked on that. It was a big bust. A *fatal* error. We spent a fair amount of time on it, sold it, and then had to apologize for *years* after that. It was an application that was released before its time. The hardware was not nearly powerful enough to run such a database. Microseed executed logically and did its job, but you could take a long nap before it could solve a realistic problem." Although it did not set Microsoft back much financially, it was a headache in terms of marketing and relationships: "Because we sold them a program that didn't work well, we essentially had an IOU out to the customers who bought it." Indeed, Microseed was ahead of its time. Eventually Microsoft did get back into the database business with products such as Access and SQL, and the company continues to do well in that area.

About the same time, IBM and Microsoft had meetings to define what IBM's PC should be. Bob says, "We met with them a number of times and discussed different aspects. We discussed whether to go with the 8080 or the 8086." Bill Gates preferred the 8086 chip. It had a 1-megabyte capacity and was much faster. "We had just planned to sell our languages to IBM and then they could get the operating system from Digital Research. Bill set up an appointment for the two of them to meet. It did not go well. For some reason or reasons, IBM decided they did not want to work with Digital. IBM wanted *us* to take responsibility for the operating system," Bob says.

No one had any inkling that this would be a turning point for Microsoft. When Microsoft agreed in 1980 to write and create an operating system for IBM, it was a huge task for Bob. Bob was *the* programmer for this joint venture. IBM would use the 8088 chip, which acted like the 8086 but was slower. At first, instead of working on the operating system itself, Microsoft simply decided to find a vendor for IBM. Tim Patterson at Seattle Computer Products, which had worked on the 8086 hardware, had written a crude operating system called QDOS (Quick and Dirty OS) to show off his hardware. Microsoft reached an agreement with Seattle Computer Products to acquire the rights to QDOS. It became Bob's job to turn QDOS into an operating system for IBM. That would become MS-DOS. About three-fourths of the way into the project, Microsoft hired Tim Patterson, who was adept at both hardware and software.

Bob was in charge of the MS-DOS development and went to work as soon as he received the first prototype of the IBM PC during the Thanksgiving 1980 weekend. Bob worked 18 hours a day, day in and day out, even on Christmas and New Year's Day, bringing up DOS on the IBM PC. Although IBM delivered developmental hardware and software, Bob found a lot of problems with the IBM hardware. He says, "I was trying to make software work on the prototype PC and it wouldn't work as advertised. I'd try to write to the disk but the printer would respond or funny things like that. I was just desperate to get things to work and it just drove me nuts! Sometimes things would work and sometimes they wouldn't. The explanation I usually got was that they used wire-wrapped logic at the time. There were physical wires between the posts. As the prototype would heat up, they'd release and the current would not run well between them. It was maddening. You've got enough problems with software that you don't trust anyway. You don't need hardware problems, too." IBM sent representatives to help Bob with the hardware problems. "They were very helpful," says Bob. "Nevertheless, if I phoned them and no one was there who could answer my questions, then I'd have to try and solve combinations of hardware and software problems myself. I'd be banging my head against the wall for days on what should have been simple little easy problems."

Bob spent long days working through the difficulties. He says, "It's hard to describe how I worked on it. I had one computer that was a prototype from IBM and another from Intel, which was a production machine with their software on it. I'd put an 'umbilical' cord between the two machines and see what happened, instruction by instruction. Seattle Computer Products would give me an eight-inch disk of their work. I would couple that with the software I had written to make the rudiments of the operating system work on the IBM PC. I'd move that over to the PC and test it out. I'd use the Intel computer to help me diagnose problems. They were usually hardware problems. So, if I was *awake,* I was working. I was single at the time so I didn't have a lot of distractions."

IBM asked Microsoft to observe complete security and secrecy as they worked together on the project. They expected Bob to work behind locked doors, and the heat in the small room would often get to Bob. "But," he adds, "there's no better feeling than the first time a program runs and executes correctly and solves the problem. It's a fabulous feeling."

Being project leader and sole programmer bringing up DOS on the IBM PC was Bob's final technical project for Microsoft. He is very proud of that project, and rightly so.

It changed the face of the computer industry forever and made Microsoft a Fortune 500 company.

In 1980, Microsoft had 40 employees and by 1982 had nearly 200 employees. Because no one at Microsoft or IBM foresaw what their joint venture would bring, Bob and others had no hint of the company's future phenomenal success. Bob smiles and says, "I thought when I joined in 1977 that we'd be successful if we got to forty or fifty people. I thought if we pulled together we could be successful." He shrugs his shoulders and laughs. "In the early days, *nobody* had a clue. *Bill* didn't have any more of a clue than *I* did. I remember talking to Bill when he was trying to talk me into leaving Albuquerque to move to Bellevue. I wasn't too crazy about the idea. I just didn't know where the company was headed. Bill said, 'Hey, it's not like we're trying to be IBM or something.' I always remembered that specific comment. There were too many factors out of our control at the time. Who would have thought that an Intel Pentium II would run at 500 megahertz and people would have 250 megabytes of memory on their PC computers? Nobody would have dreamed of it! That would have been more powerful than the mainframes that were around at the time.

"The roots of Microsoft are in computer languages. The fantastic success of the operating system occurred because the stars came into alignment," says Bob. During that time, Intel was making progress with the microprocessor. Memory became cheap and available to the microcomputer. Good graphics were available as well as large and fast disk drives. When Bob came into the business, there were no hard drives on microcomputers. Of course, the significance of software shortly fell into place within the industry and within companies such as Microsoft. The information technology revolution was gathering steam. "Microsoft was built piece by piece," Bob points out.

After the IBM PC came out in 1981, Bob moved to sales and marketing and eventually to administration. His first position was as an original equipment manufacturer (OEM) sales and accounts manager in the United States. Bob would visit Xerox, Texas Instruments, and other companies that were incorporating Microsoft software into their hardware and then reselling it. In early 1982, he became the international accounts manager. Scott Oki had just come on board, and Microsoft International was to be his brainchild.

Bob moved to Europe to open up Microsoft offices. His base was London. With amazement, Bob remembers, "I was a guy who had never been to Europe and my first trip there is to set up offices!" Scott Oki was concentrating on Japan and was appointed VP of Microsoft International. Bob and Scott worked closely together. They changed the strategy of having a single European headquarters in England to having separate subsidiaries in England, France, and Germany. This created a huge recruiting problem for Bob and Scott. They needed to find the right people to run those subsidiaries: marketing, sales, technical, and distribution staffs.

Bob faced many challenges while setting up international offices and ended up spending 18 months living in Europe. There were different employment issues and customs in each country. Bob notes, "There were different vacation requirements. Should a person have a company car? Each culture was different. In France you had Napoleonic law. Ergonomics was of paramount importance in Germany, so we had to have certain types of desks and windows." Bob laughs, "And in England, I don't think anybody cared!"

Fortunately, at the time, Microsoft did not have a lot of bureaucracy. Bob recalls, "The thing that really stunned me the most was when we finally got a lawyer to look at our OEM contracts. That really put a halt as to how fast I could do any new contracts. I had a good technical background—I knew the products quite well and the OEM contracts. I'd go on and negotiate and maybe make a few changes. I'd call Bill or someone at headquarters and ask if we could do something. Then I'd send the contract to Bill. He'd sign it and away we'd go! It worked really smoothly until we got lawyers involved. It really slowed things down. But in all fairness to the lawyers, we probably were creating a lot of liabilities." In the early days at Microsoft, Bob, Bill, and others wrote their own contracts because the business was so new and no one—certainly no lawyer—knew it as well as they did.

At the time, e-mail was available only at headquarters in Bellevue. Recalls Bob, "I wrote an enormous amount of telexes." Bill and Paul made several trips to Europe to check on the progress. Bob says quietly, "It was on a trip to Paris that Paul Allen became very ill. After returning to the United States, he was diagnosed with Hodgkin's disease." Paul took time off from the company and eventually got well.

Bob was traveling most of the time. Scott was traveling constantly. Bob and others referred to Scott Oki as "The Force." "He had this enormous energy. He'd be in Tokyo one day and back at headquarters the next. He had the energy to keep us all going, and he was full of new information. It was incredible the way he could keep up with things. He was an extremely organized guy. He was really great to work with."

One of Bob's jobs was to interview people. He had a strategy for selecting the right person. He says, "I wanted every person I hired to be as smart or smarter than I was.

If I didn't feel that way about a person, I'd just keep looking. It just made sense to me. That was the only way the company was going to progress. I compromised that idea on a few occasions and regretted it."

From 1982 on, Bob had a number of titles, among them International Accounts Manager, Intercontinental Business Development Manager, Director of Intercontinental Operations, and Director of Subsidiary Development. Bob is extremely proud of the people he hired. Among them were Bernard Vergnes, chairman of the board of Europe; Linda Graham and David Svendsen of Australia; Gregorio Diaz, director of Latin America; and Orlando Ayala, senior VP of International. Many more of Bob's hires attained high levels within the company. "One of my key achievements at Microsoft was hiring good people," he says.

When Bob developed the Intercontinental Business Division in 1983, he worked in Australia, Latin America, Canada, and the Middle East. In Australia and Canada he set up front offices. In the remaining countries he set up distribution centers. Later he set up businesses in Africa, Mexico, and India. Bob managed the general managers. He was responsible for approximately 150 people. At Microsoft, many people with specialized skills rather than business backgrounds were asked to become managers. Bob says, "It's hard. I don't think I was ever a natural manager. It wasn't a natural fit for me. But I did it. It's painful from time to time. I really disliked working with my staff on their reviews. It's very hard for me to criticize people. I had to do it. But I *hated* it."

Although Bob dislikes confrontation, there were times when he and Bill would really get into what Bob terms "a very heated debate." Early on, Bob and Bill had argued about the work on BASIC. "It wasn't as fast as we all wanted it to be. We'd look at some of the key routines and debate, instruction by instruction, how that routine should work. There were a few times that Gates and I were at odds on that. We'd take it down to the nitty-gritty to see who was right," Bob says. If the debate was too heated, Bob would regain his emotional equilibrium rather quickly: "I'd just go home and get a good night's sleep." Bob muses for a moment and continues. "If they could make the project better, then I'd be the better for it. We all had a little bit of ownership. Bill and Paul oversaw everything we did. No product was developed in isolation. There were plenty of critics around."

In 1993, after 16 years with Microsoft, Bob decided to retire. "I'd had retirement in the back of my mind for several years," Bob says. "We had some strong regional offices, and they were quite capable. I guess you could say I worked myself out of a job. The offices had all the skills they needed. So I started to look around to see what else I might want to do at Microsoft. I just didn't find anything I could get excited about. I didn't want to manage people anymore. I'd had enough of that!

"The growth of Microsoft has been different every year. It's quite different now. I was more of a small company type of person. As a company grows larger, you have to have controls. But most large companies reach a point where bureaucracy becomes inevitable. Microsoft is probably a saint in those regards. They probably have the least bureaucracy. They give people a piece of the action so that they feel they have some control over a project. I have tremendous confidence in the company because Bill and Paul and Steve are still running it."

Despite his many accomplishments and savvy business acumen, Bob still has a sense of wonder about his 16 years at Microsoft. He says with genuine enthusiasm, "Microsoft was just so much fun. It went by so fast!"

Life after Microsoft

"I always wanted to do something with my brother," Bob says. So in 1985 the two of them started a ranch in the Texas Panhandle where they grew up. Because Bob enjoys farming equipment but not the animals, his brother runs and operates the ranch. Bob provides the financing and the business structure. Although ranching is an extremely expensive and risky enterprise, the brothers enjoy it. Freed from the demanding environment of Microsoft, Bob now has more time for his family, golf, racquetball, and skiing.

Bob is a director on the boards of several local businesses. He also invests in real estate development. Just before Bob retired, he joined an advisory council for the College of Natural Sciences at the University of Texas, his alma mater. He helps the working relationship between the university and Microsoft by encouraging Microsoft to recruit students from the university.

Bob is careful to keep his life as uncomplicated as possible. As for being wealthy, he says, "Sometimes possessions own you as much as you own them. I try to keep that to a minimum. If all my money went away tomorrow," Bob says, "I'd find some way of getting by."

SCOTT OKI

"The Force"

Microsoft: 1982–1992

Vice President, International

Senior Vice President, United States

SCOTT OKI

"The Force"

Scott Oki, a quietly handsome Japanese-American, is charismatic, well mannered, and a gifted public speaker. An avid golfer, he dresses in casual clothes. As his nickname suggests, he approaches every endeavor, whether business or philanthropy, with enormous enthusiasm.

Scott was the founder of Microsoft International. He had the foresight to see in the early 1980s that the world market was being left fallow by other software companies entering and competing in the technological revolution. His major achievement was putting Microsoft on the global map.

When the domestic division of Microsoft was replete with problems and red ink, Bill Gates asked Scott to move from International to become senior vice president of the company's U.S. domestic division. Scott went in and fixed things. In a few years, U.S. Domestic was back on track and reaping profits.

Because of his passion and work ethic, his coworkers at Microsoft called him "The Force."

The Path to Microsoft

Scott Oki was born into a time and culture that did not encourage taking risks. His parents, like thousands of other Japanese-Americans in the early 1940s, were forced to spend World War II in crowded, barren, and guarded compounds known as internment camps. They lost everything—their homes, their businesses, their livelihoods, and most of their possessions. It was a humiliating experience that left a lasting impression on Scott, and it shaped his upbringing. His parents, he says, "encouraged us to take a safer path, and that safer path was getting a college education and working in a profession as a doctor, a lawyer, or an engineer. Once you're educated, you're educated. It can't be taken away from you." Although his father had studied chemical engineering, after the war he worked for the U.S. Postal Service. Scott's mother worked as a secretary for the Federal Housing Administration. Scott says, "As paradoxical as that may seem, my parents needed secure and safe jobs. Prior to the war, most Japanese-Americans were entrepreneurs."

After the war, Scott was raised in a three-room tenement in Seattle's Chinatown, now known as the International District. He remembers it well. "We had to use a public rest room to bathe." In spite of the environment, Scott credits his parents with his striving for excellence in all that he did, whether it was judo, Boy Scouts, school, or playing the saxophone. The entire community supported this kind of work ethic. Scott says, "We were always involved in the community. It was a great safety net and support structure for us when we were growing up."

It was Scott's father who decided Scott would become an electrical engineer. Scott really didn't know what he wanted to be, but as a dutiful Japanese-American son, he honored his father's wishes. At Franklin High School, located in a culturally and economically diverse neighborhood, Scott took all the accelerated science classes. He did extremely well, and when he graduated, he thought his career path was determined. At the University of Washington, Scott majored in electrical engineering, but says, "I wasn't a very good student." Eventually he decided to explore new territory. "The thing that was kind of a watershed for me was actually leaving Seattle," Scott says. "If I hadn't left, I think that I would be a far different person than I am currently. It was being thrust out of that very *comfortable*, that very *safe* existence in the Japanese-American community that forced me to think differently about things, to gain new experiences, to be out there on my own—to get outside of my comfort zone and to take some risks. I found that I *liked* it."

In 1969, when Scott was 21 years old, he joined the Air Force. He was stationed in Colorado and began to take college courses at the University of Colorado. He graduated magna cum laude in 1974 with majors in information systems and accounting and was the top graduate in his MBA class. With his MBA in hand, Scott went to work in marketing for Hewlett-Packard's Colorado Springs and Fort Collins Divisions and the General Systems Division in Cupertino, California. Although he did quite well there, he was eager to strike out on his own. He was ready to take more risks, challenge himself, and test his abilities.

In 1980, he decided to start a software company, Sequoia Group, in San Francisco. The company developed a turnkey system—hardware and software—for doctors' offices. It was used for back-office accounting. Scott did everything: product marketing, testing, development, and customer service. But, in spite of all his passion and hard work, he and his partners could not agree on the future plan for the company. Scott decided to leave. Without knowing it, Scott was on a career path that would shortly lead him to Microsoft. He was undaunted by his failed start-up. "It was that experience, that pure start-up experience that whetted my appetite for more. The school of hard knocks is probably the best preparation for a career in corporate America," Scott says.

After the failure of his company, Scott stayed in San Francisco and did some consulting work for a very successful company, MicroPro. It was the dominant software applications company at that time and growing very rapidly. Seymour Rubenstein, the founder, asked Scott and his partner, Michael Rothschild, to do a very high level strategic consulting project. Scott says, "It was almost a blank sheet of paper; there really wasn't a specific focus. But in most consulting projects, examining your competition is a significant part in influencing what kind of recommendations you'll make." That's when Scott first heard of Microsoft. "During the research phase of that consulting project I kept running up against Microsoft. I didn't know anything about the company. I became very intrigued because the company had located in Bellevue, Washington, and I'm a native of Seattle. I wondered why a software company would be out in the boonies," Scott says and laughs. At that time, most of the software giants were located in the Silicon Valley and in Boston along the Route 128 corridor.

Microsoft intrigued Scott for a number of reasons. First, he thought the company's strategy was extremely smart. Second, it had a dominant share in the computer-language business. "The data I uncovered showed that they were starting to get into operating systems with Soft-Card that Paul Allen had invented. In addition, there was also a lot of talk about Microsoft developing a strategy to develop applications software products. It just seemed so smart to me," says Scott. Although Microsoft was then known in the industry as a computer-language company, it was branching out into the design of software applications, for which a market was just emerging. Each computer can use only one operating system, but Microsoft had its eye on another, potentially immense market. Scott notes, "You can sell more than one application software product for each computer. That was just so gutsy. Who knew whether or not they really had the resources to pull it off? Obviously, it's a lot more difficult to be competitive in all those businesses rather than just focusing on one."

More and more curious about Microsoft, Scott wrote a letter to Bill Gates. Bill forwarded the letter to Steve Ballmer, then VP of corporate staffing. Steve looked at Scott's resume and noticed the name of his start-up company, Sequoia Group. He remembered a friend of his, Michael Goldberg, mentioning the company. As luck would have it, Michael was also a friend of Scott's. Scott laughs as he recounts the serendipity involved. "Ballmer called Michael in San Francisco and said, 'Hey, do you know anything about this Scott Oki guy?'" Michael put in a good word for Scott, and in 1982 Scott was invited to Bellevue for a series of interviews with Microsoft.

At the same time, Scott had other offers to consider, including one from MicroPro. However, during his research for MicroPro, Scott and others had recommended to Seymour Rubenstein that he lay off half of his workforce. Scott notes, "That's pretty significant. It's a very painful process. Microsoft was hiring, not laying off." Besides, Scott missed doing entrepreneurial things. MicroPro could not offer him that. Scott says that although he wasn't particularly interested in returning to Seattle, he took the job at Microsoft because "it had all the advantages of a start-up and none of the baggage. Baggage is going out and raising money and paying attention to the people who provide the capital. At Microsoft, one person was making the decisions—Bill." Scott also believed that even though MicroPro was the dominant company at the time, Microsoft was in better position to exploit the software applications market and that the software future belonged to the company in the "boonies."

Life at Microsoft

Although the compensation package offered Scott was less attractive than MicroPro's, Scott joined Microsoft in 1982. He says, "My gut told me that they were going to be more successful than MicroPro." Scott's failed start-up, Sequoia Group, had taught him that wealth was not going to be built from the size of one's paycheck. Scott says, "I felt that fortunes would be made from stock options, and I held true to that. Every opportunity I had, I would forgo salary increases or I would take a much smaller increase. I'd tell Bill that what I really wanted was more stock options. In hindsight, I guess that was a pretty smart trade-off."

In early 1982, Microsoft had approximately 120 employees. It was an energetic and creative time for the company and for Scott. He liked the entrepreneurial environment. He says, "I spent the first month bouncing around the halls trying to figure out what it was I really wanted to do." He'd been given the job title of Marketing Manager of Special Accounts, which included the IBM Personal Computer Division located in Boca Raton. A second account, Lifeboat Associates, located in New York, was Microsoft's largest distributor of its retail products. A third was Microsoft's agency relationship in Japan, ASCII. These three accounts represented a significant portion of Microsoft's revenue streams and profits. IBM was especially important because it had the ability to influence whether other computer manufacturers would widely adopt Microsoft's operating system, MS-DOS, as the industry standard.

Given the situation then and the way the businesses had been set up, Scott says, "I soon realized there was no way I could do a good job at all three of these things." The businesses were three separate entities, and Scott felt that International was a far better opportunity for Microsoft.

Scott got focused. He pondered what the biggest opportunity was for Microsoft. Having come from Hewlett-Packard, he understood what an international presence meant. Foreign sales had represented 40 percent of HP's business. Scott says, "I always remembered that. I thought there was a huge opportunity that no one was looking at. International was just being sorely neglected—it was basically lying fallow. But Microsoft had a lot of company in this regard." Virtually all of the software companies were concentrating on U.S. sales.

During the next month, Scott wrote a business plan to set up Microsoft International. He identified the largest market opportunities—France, the United Kingdom, and Germany—and recommended starting wholly owned subsidiaries for each market rather than setting up a single European headquarters. He also wanted to have distribution centers around the world. Although he had faith in his plan and his ability, he knew he was taking a huge risk. There were no guidelines to follow—no one in the nascent PC software industry had done it successfully before. Fortunately, Microsoft was still a small company and it was fairly easy to set goals and achieve them. Bureaucracy was virtually nonexistent. Scott smiles and recalls, "There was not a lot of process. You could communicate orally—you didn't have to write a lot of things down or document things." So when Scott presented Bill Gates with his business plan it caught everyone off guard. Scott says, "No one was used to reviewing a formal business plan. Bill was astounded when I presented the plan to him. Back in the early days it was pretty gross, just the rudimentary sorts of things we were doing."

As part of his business plan, Scott asked Bill for $1 million in capitalization. In return, Scott would start three wholly owned subsidiaries in Europe in addition to the one in Japan, and he would manage all the business outside of the U.S. domestic market. In 1982, $1 million was a huge sum of money for Microsoft. But Bill told Scott, "Yeah, okay, go do it." Scott believed that the sooner they got into a market and erected competitive barriers the better off they'd be. Clearly, he was putting himself and his future on the line. "I had made some bold promises to Bill, but I delivered," he says. In fact, he promised Bill that International would achieve profitability and cash-flow breakeven within just one year. He also promised to establish MS-DOS as the standard in the international market, which was much more difficult than doing so in the United States. Scott says proudly, "Every subsidiary we started was essentially cash-flow positive within one year. But," Scott also points out, "I did not write a five-year plan that said we would experience the kind of growth we did."

Scott's imprint was all over Microsoft International. His face brightens and he speaks with great enthusiasm. "International was a pure start-up experience. I wrote the rules. I hired the people. I established the 'culture' for each subsidiary so it would look, feel, and work like the mother ship in Bellevue. It was my creation. The U.S. side of the house was an existing thing. International was a real adventure for me. I had the entire world in my hands. I had the freedom to make decisions and implement plans without anyone looking too closely over my shoulder. It all has to do with market preemption, having a good product, being a good salesman, and hiring great people. The only vision was that there was this huge untapped market. I didn't know *anything* about the international marketplace when I began, but I'm not afraid of hard work. I'm reasonably intelligent and I just thought I'd figure it out."

His peers called Scott "The Force" during those years. He traveled constantly and seemed inexhaustible. "One doesn't amass the frequent flyer miles I did by sitting in Bellevue." In 1984, he was Pan Am's number one frequent flyer. When he boarded a flight from Sydney to Los Angeles, the flight attendants greeted him with the news. "They actually had it on their manifest," Scott recalls, shaking his head and chuckling. "That year I had flown 400,000 miles—just on one carrier!"

Scott explains how he accomplished so much in so little time and how he kept his energy going: "You have to be a good manager of time. If I was traveling the transpacific or the polar route, I was on the plane at least ten hours. There's time to sleep. If I was in a taxi going from one meeting to another, I'd sleep." Professional time managers didn't talk about sleep. Nor did they talk about the kind of commitment Scott had made.

"In my first few years with Microsoft I didn't take a single day off. I was in the office sending e-mail on Christmas Day. No one else was there, but I was there." He has no complaints. "It was hard work, but I think, like anything, if you're having fun doing it—if you're just totally passionate about it—you don't mind the hours."

Some of Scott's colleagues were concerned that he would have difficulty succeeding in Europe. People told him that the European work ethic was far different from the work ethic at Microsoft. "I didn't quite understand why that would be," Scott says. "I mean, people are people. I don't know how somebody can stereotype a culture in terms of a work ethic. Obviously, you need to hire the right people. I wanted to find the ones who would work harder than others do and set an example for Microsoft International. I also looked for people who had start-up experience. I didn't care whether they were successful or failed start-ups." He looked for people who were risk takers and who had high energy levels. In fact, Scott told prospective employees exactly what he was looking for. "I was searching for people who were looking for an opportunity to prove something—people who wanted to be the king or queen of their respective country. I even characterized it that way," says Scott, with a laugh. Imagine doing that in the United States.

The first 10 general managers Scott hired had start-up experience. He spent long hours hiring the country managers, working with them, training them, and educating them. "It required just being there. I would work with them from seven in the morning until midnight," Scott recalls. Again, his commitment of time to the job was extraordinary.

Competition also played a role in the success of International. Scott notes, "External competition is certainly effective. It's an easy way to motivate people. It's a way for them to associate with the greater goal. You could point to Digital Research, Lotus, or VisiCorp in the old days—or whoever—as the bad guys. It's *easy* to compete against the bad guys when you see yourself as the white knight in the whole thing." Winning became a matter of pride in a job well done, and it was raised almost to a moral level. Losing to a competitor was to lose credibility, and the company's sense of its own worth was at stake. Inevitably, mistakes were made. But unlike many other companies, when Microsoft International employees made mistakes, they accepted the blame and learned from them. This reinforced their sense of mission. "Losing a few battles was grudgingly accommodated. Losing a war was *unthinkable,*" says Scott.

After finding the right people, Scott had his work cut out for him. Establishing MS-DOS as the standard in the international market was much more difficult than doing so in the United States. In the United States, IBM had been setting standards in the mainframe market, and as soon as it chose MS-DOS as its operating system, DOS also became the de facto standard in the U.S. industry.

Doing an operating system for IBM was not something that was a natural extension for Microsoft. When IBM reps first approached Microsoft, Bill Gates sent them to Digital Research. Digital wasn't interested. Scott explains, "I think Bill, in the early days, was primarily interested in writing language compilers. There was BASIC, COBOL, FORTRAN, or Pascal. The company had created a comfortable existence in a niche market—computer languages. Bill is, by nature, a very opportunistic guy, but we got pulled almost kicking and screaming into the operating systems business." The operating systems business ended up being a huge cash cow and funded all the future investments the company would make in the applications business.

But in the international markets, hardware OEMs were uninterested in licensing MS-DOS. "The thought of manufacturing an IBM PC clone was anathema to their very existence," says Scott. At that time, most PC OEMs preferred to use different operating systems, such as CP/M, an operating system by Digital Research. CP/M was quite active and dominant in the PC market. This presented a big problem for Microsoft. "So, we had the additional challenge of overcoming those resistance points, and they were not insignificant. They were very, very large resistance points. We finally ended up winning the battle through just plain hard work and salesmanship," says Scott.

Once the international hardware manufacturers licensed the operating system, Microsoft took advantage of that fact by then licensing localized applications software to them. Ironically, getting into that business led Microsoft into all of its other businesses. Scott notes, "Those were *huge*, I mean unbelievably large revenue producers— income streams that continued to fuel International at the time, and no one from either company foresaw what this partnership would mean to Microsoft and later to IBM."

Scott also had some tough decisions to make regarding Microsoft's agency relationship in Japan. In Japan, Kay Nishi, who ran ASCII, was considered to be a whiz kid. Nishi was the Bill Gates of Japan. When Bill went to Japan he would see Nishi and discuss things high tech. Their relationship had been established before Scott joined Microsoft. At that time, many of the hardware innovations were coming out of Japan, and when Bill traveled there he'd meet with the representatives from the semiconductor, CD-ROM, laser printers, and display industries. "I think, more than anything, that gave Bill a unique window on all the different products and innovations impacting the high-tech world and a view as to how quickly platforms would emerge. It was hugely beneficial for Bill, and he still does that research," says Scott.

Scott says, "Kay Nishi had the same reputation in Japan as Bill did in the United States. He was unique. He could influence the hardware manufacturers there just like Bill could influence Compaq or IBM. Kay did a great job, and he was very much an entrepreneur. But he didn't believe in a lot of financial controls. I was there to leverage and maximize Microsoft's presence in Japan and elsewhere in the world while applying financial discipline."

It quickly became clear to Scott that the agency relationship in Japan was not going to work for the long-term good of the company. Scott recommended to Bill that they establish their own wholly owned subsidiary. There were repercussions from this decision. Scott chooses his words carefully. "If Kay wanted to work as an employee of Microsoft, obviously he would be working for me on at least a dotted-line relationship. It would be hard to accept that. Sam Furukawa, Kay's right-hand man at ASCII, came to work for Microsoft Japan. He brought with him a dozen ASCII employees, and they formed the nucleus of what is now the largest and most profitable subsidiary at Microsoft." Scott adds, "It was a very painful divorce. A very, very messy affair."

In 1983, a year after putting his business plan into action, Scott was named vice president of Microsoft International. He was 34 years old, and his name was synonymous with Microsoft International. He absolutely loved what he was doing. "When I get focused, nothing else matters. Doing International—that's what I was living and breathing. I was determined to be successful. I'd been through a failed start-up and I learned from those mistakes and the accumulated scar tissue. I'm a very competitive individual. I didn't let anything get in the way." As a result, International was an amazing success, generating huge sums of money through a network of dozens of wholly owned subsidiaries, joint ventures, agency relationships, and distributors in every part of the world. Within four years, the division accounted for 42 percent of Microsoft's revenue and greater than 50 percent of the company's profits.

It is truly an amazing success story that put Microsoft on the global map. Contributing to this success were innovative pricing strategies that were totally different from those in the U.S. market. Scott speaks frankly.

"Basically, we were charging what the United States thought were *unbelievable* amounts for our software and getting away with it."

Scott and those in International were responsible for selling localized versions of MS-DOS, Multiplan, Chart, and all other Microsoft products. The goal was to establish MS-DOS as the standard in the international marketplace. "Each country had its own language, customs, business practices, laws, and currencies. Everything was different. We managed to extract some extremely favorable OEM agreements not only for operating systems and language compilers, but also for applications software. The first thing I ever sold was a multimillion-dollar agreement with AppleEurope for localized versions of Multiplan running on the Apple IIE. That provided the capitalization and fueled our growth," says Scott.

Multiplan, Microsoft's first application software, had disappointing sales in the United States, but it was a huge hit in Europe and the number one–selling spreadsheet in France. Multiplan became synonymous with the term *spreadsheet.* Then the first version of Microsoft Word came out in 1983, and by 1987, Word 3.0 was a huge success in France. The sales and marketing people Scott hired in France were extremely dedicated. When Word first came out, they visited all the distributors in the country and trained them on Word. In addition, OEMs agreed to include packaged products with each computer sold. When clones of the IBM PC, such as Compaq, came out, the manufacturers had to license MS-DOS from Microsoft.

Scott accidentally discovered the market potential of Australia. Scott set up Microsoft there in a rather roundabout way. He had just set up the Munich, Paris, and London subsidiaries on the seed money that Bill had given him. He had some money left from the $1 million.

Scott believed the timing and price were right to buy out their exclusive distributor in Australia and start a whole new subsidiary. Scott says, "It wasn't because of this strategic thing that said we were gonna make a gazillion dollars in Australia! There were bigger and more important markets than that. It was convenient, and the idea resonated with Linda and Richard Graham, the owners of Wiser Microsoft. Linda agreed to become the country manager for Microsoft Australia." Scott could see that buying out a well-established distributorship in Australia just made good business sense. Scott attributes Microsoft's great success in Australia to luck, but those who watched International's phenomenal growth suspect that his uncanny instinct for being in the right place at the right time played a large role.

Unfortunately, Microsoft U.S. Domestic Sales Division was ailing and badly in need of help. Bill Gates turned to Scott in 1986 and persuaded him to leave International. Bill's persuasion took the form of more stock options and a promotion to senior VP of U.S. sales and marketing. Scott was flattered that Bill had so much trust in him. Although International had been almost his whole life for four years, because Scott felt confidence in his staff, he took on the challenge of U.S. Domestic. Scott recalls, "While I was running International, the U.S. side of the house was an existing thing, and replete with problems. They had always had problems. I mean, huge problems. It was a horrible situation. They were losing money hand over fist. That was one of the reasons Bill wanted me to come across." Microsoft's growth, coupled with multiple businesses and products in segments saturated with well-entrenched competitors, had stretched the company much too thin. Bill had trusted his U.S. executives to mind the store. When he realized the store was badly leaking red ink, he was lucky to have Scott to turn to. Bill trusted Scott because of his outstanding performance in International. And Scott felt equal to the challenge.

So, four years after founding International, Scott became senior VP of domestic sales and marketing. "I was kind of a hired gun who had to go in and clean house and get things tracking to profitability. I needed to reinvigorate that division. This was a very different challenge for me. It wasn't a start-up, but an existing and broken organization." How did Microsoft Domestic become such a mess? "I don't think they hired very good people with the attributes that I was accustomed to in Microsoft International," Scott says. "Certainly there were some who were really great, but the vast majority didn't cut my acid test. I coined the phrase 'maniacal work ethic' because so many people at Microsoft work so hard."

Even though Microsoft was very careful about hiring, Scott found a far different culture had developed in Domestic than in International. Scott says, "When we'd have a sales meeting in International, people would work really hard. In going to a sales meeting in Domestic U.S., people were partying." Scott shakes his head at the memory and says, "I thought that was really strange. And there wasn't as much product knowledge and expertise as I had come to expect. How much can you attribute to the fact that some of the products weren't very good?" Although Multiplan, one of the very good products, had become a leader in International it was an also-ran in the U.S. marketplace. Scott says, "Part of the problem was trying to recruit people in the United States—these people had many choices." In fact, they could work for one of the many U.S. companies such as VisiCorp, Software Publishing, Lotus, WordPerfect, Ashton-Tate, Borland, and others. People didn't have these kinds of opportunities in International. Scott ran International with an ever present eye on the work ethic and the culture. He says,

"We really took an attitude of preempting competition, investing in localizing products, erecting barriers to entry, and we took these things very seriously. We worked amazingly hard to put those things in place." Scott was extremely protective of his organization and culture. "I didn't want expatriate Americans working in our subsidiaries," he notes. "I wanted those subsidiaries to be 100 percent local nationals—to be run by natives. I was maniacal about that."

U.S. Domestic had about 26 sales offices when Scott inherited the division. He closed down about half of them. But Scott was not a callous downsizer. He took personal responsibility and accountability for every firing and rehiring. He spent a good deal of time and energy during the process. "I met with and interviewed every single person in the sales organization. After a brief conversation, I'd know who the keepers were. I decided to 'reboot' the sales organization, and that's what we did. I don't think anyone likes firing people or downsizing or redeploying resources or whatever the phrase of the month happens to be. It's a very emotional thing. It's very time-consuming, but sometimes very necessary."

Then they rehired. "We hired great people who were in the mold of who we thought we should have. This was the place to start," Scott explains. More important, he had an acid test for these people. He was looking for particular qualities. He asked himself, "Are they passionate about the business?" He would look for indications of their work ethic. "Some of them would just put you to sleep. It was just a job. I wasn't looking for people who wanted a job or a paycheck. I wanted to know how hard they worked, how big their batteries were and how often they needed recharging, how smart they were, how articulate they were, how much bandwidth they had between their ears," Scott notes. Obviously, given International's successful staff, Scott had a talent for reading an applicant's prospective worth to the company. By 1990, within four years, the U.S. division was back in the black in a dramatic way, achieving a whopping 20 percent profit before taxes and sales revenues of over $1 billion, up from $100 million in less than five years.

From his very first day at Microsoft, Scott understood what it would take to succeed in such a high-energy, self-critical, and confrontational company. He understood why Bill and others saw it as a way to manage the company. "There's no one more confrontational than Bill, so it starts at the top," says Scott. "You have to understand the nature of the beast, so to speak." Scott pauses, thinks for a moment, and enunciates each word, "Bill has not changed his spots. It's uncanny the kinds of questions he asks, how he always gets to the soft underbelly of the issue. If you haven't done your homework, he's going to tear you apart. You learn very quickly that you'd better have your ducks in a row. You'd better be able to support your recommendations or you're going to get your head handed to you on a platter." Scott muses for a moment and laughs, "I've been handed my head on a platter by Bill a few times." He understood that at Microsoft everyone was involved in putting out the best products, and sometimes that meant criticizing an idea or a project.

Scott explains why the confrontational style worked at Microsoft in this way. "Being confrontational meant debating issues and coming up with the right answers to whatever problem you're trying to solve." When Scott ran International, he'd convene monthly meetings with his general managers. Not only did he expect them to discuss the issues, but to debate them. "The GMs would come forth with recommendations and we'd tear those recommendations apart and test the thinking and do all the things that allowed us to come up with the best decision.

It's part of the process." Scott implemented what he called, "the Great Debates" when he took over U.S. Domestic. One person would take one side of an issue and another person would take the other side. They would debate that issue in front of the entire senior management staff. Of these debates, Scott says, "People learn to become good thinkers if they weren't good thinkers before. If you were to ask people who lived through 'the Great Debates,' they would probably tell you they were the most productive and enlightening discussions they have ever been involved in.

"I think you have to be a little bit crazy to work the long hours. But it's all part of the Microsoft culture and it's not something that feels right for everyone. Those people select themselves out of the process involuntarily because they can't cut it. You have to be *focused*. There are degrees of focus, and those who want to excel and to get promoted walk the extra mile and work the extra day. Microsoft is still very much a meritocracy."

It is not surprising that Scott excelled at Microsoft, although he gives a humble assessment of himself. "There are a lot of people in the world who are smarter than me, a lot of people who work harder than me, people with a higher IQ, better looking. . . . I think what I brought to the table at the time was a focus and a passion and an uncanny knack to hire insanely great people that provided an unbelievable amount of growth, revenue, and profit for Microsoft. If I had come to Microsoft a year later and someone else was doing the international stuff, I don't know what I'd be doing. Maybe managing the IBM account or something else. The timing was right." Scott's humility is characteristic of his Japanese-American upbringing. But Scott is also a hard-core realist. He understands that he was in the right place at the right time. It's hard to imagine "The Force" as a middle manager at some other company. What Scott asked from those he hired he also asked from himself. No one is harder on Scott Oki than Scott Oki. He demands perfection and hard work from himself.

Life after Microsoft

Since Scott's retirement in 1992, he is busier than ever. An avid golfer, he recently developed what he hopes will become one of the top golf courses in the United States. He and his wife Laurie own a Japanese restaurant, Nishino. He owns commercial and residential real estate and invests in high-tech companies. He was a University of Washington regent.

Among the numerous high-technology companies Scott has invested in are 2Way Inc., A1 Inc., Children's Media Network Inc., Coinstar, DiAMAR Interactive Corporation, Key Computer, NETbot Inc., Primus Communications, Q-Point, Net Manage, Visio, Mega depot.com, Greater Good.com, and Freeshop.com.

But his real passions are developing philanthropic businesses and volunteering in various nonprofit causes. He uses Paul Newman and his charitable giving through Newman's Own products as his model for giving. Through personal experience (the birth of his second son) he learned that newborn baby blankets are not readily available. Scott and his wife Laurie decided to start a newborn baby blanket business. Blankets for newborns are given as a corporate welcoming gift to new parents. Nintendo, Boeing, Bear Stearns, Frank Russell and Company, and Microsoft are just a few of the companies who purchase blankets. Money is returned to The Oki Foundation to replenish its funds. It is then given out to various local charities that emphasize children's health and welfare.

As owner of the Seattle Sounders Soccer Team, Scott donates to the community either 100 percent of the profits or 2 percent of the ticket revenue, whichever is the greater amount.

The Okis have donated $1 million to Children's Hospital, sponsored soccer camps, given nonprofit organizations free rent in the buildings they own, and helped others start businesses. Recently Scott, along with Paul Brainerd (founder of Aldus), Ida Cole (Microsoft), Bill Neukom (Microsoft), and other high-tech millionaires, started Social Venture Partners. Individual partners contribute a minimum of $5,000 each year. The goal of SVP is to give grants as well as volunteer time and energy to local nonprofits. Their focus is on education and children's welfare. SVP gave away $500,000 its first year and $1 million in 1999.

As a Japanese-American, Scott wants to set an example. He founded the Japanese-American Chamber of Commerce and the Executive Development Institute. He is the vision behind the DENSHO project, a state-of-the-art video/oral history project on the internment of Japanese-Americans during World War II. Scott says, "I worked hard, I reached financial independence, but I *care* about what happens to someone else and to children." Scott's parents instilled these values in him by always being involved in their community. Giving back to the community is a high priority for Scott and his wife Laurie.

Scott is constantly in the spotlight; he accepts it because he wants to set an example for other minorities. He founded the Japanese-American Chamber of Commerce because he wanted to pair the sometimes-stereotypical humbleness of Asians with being visible, vocal, and taking credit for their accomplishments. But Scott says, "People don't have to change their personalities or be into personal aggrandizement."

Scott's personal mission statement is "to marry my passion for things entrepreneurial with things philanthropic in a way that encourages others to do the same."

In addition, Scott serves on two dozen nonprofit boards, including Children's Hospital, United Way of America, University of Colorado Foundation, Seattle King County Sports and Events Council, Boy Scouts, the Japanese-American Chamber of Commerce, and Fred Hutchinson Cancer Research.

Why is Scott busier than ever in retirement? He replies, "It's the same reason why I was who I was at Microsoft— it's just my nature. It's not my nature to put my feet up on the table and snooze all day. It's not me. I'm not afraid of putting blood, sweat, and tears into something I believe in."

If he had it to do all over again, would he join Microsoft? He laughs and says, "At the same age? In a second! Now? I'm too old and too tired." But actions speak louder than words. "The Force" is still very much with us.

RICHARD BRODIE

"The Dilettante"

———————■———————

Microsoft: 1981–1994

Chief Programmer

RICHARD BRODIE

"The Dilettante"

Richard Brodie is an easygoing and extremely brilliant man who has yet to reach the age of 40. His contribution to Microsoft's success has been enormous, but he seems grateful to be free of the corporate world so that he can enthusiastically pursue the many things that capture his intellectual interest. He confesses to being a dilettante.

Richard dresses elegantly but informally in slacks and a wool sweater. His slightly receding hairline highlights his friendly smile and his warm, inquisitive eyes. He is a man who is full of ideas that range from the whimsical to the deeply serious.

Richard Brodie is best known for writing the first version of Microsoft Word. He is considered one of the top programmers of our time. When Microsoft's marketing department was concerned that writing software to allow users of the first version of Word to take advantage of the newly developed "mouse" would delay the shipment of its product, Richard protested and promised to do the necessary work in no more than a week. It took him three days.

Although Richard has left Microsoft five times, Bill Gates says the door is always open if Richard decides to return.

The Path to Microsoft

Growing up in Boston in the 1960s, Richard was very fortunate to have a mother who understood his brilliance and encouraged it. When he was only seven years old, his mother purchased a plastic computer from the Mr. Wizard Shop. The computer was called Digi-Comp I. Richard says, "This was a computer with three *bits* of memory. You could represent numbers from zero to seven. It had a manual clock and you could only get it to do things once per second, one hertz." (The clocks on computers today operate in megahertz, or millionths of a second.) As primitive as this machine was, Richard was hooked. He made a program that mimicked the changing of traffic lights— 0 was off and 1 was on.

Richard says, "My mother's mission in life was to make it possible to pursue my interests. As soon as she even got a hint that I was interested in anything, then she'd make it accessible to me." She bought logic puzzles from *Scientific American.* She also taught Richard how to do Boolean algebra with punch cards and knitting needles. Richard smiles and says, "Looking at the average mom, I would say mine was remarkable. She had amazing patience for my learning."

Both of Richard's parents were mental health specialists who had been educated at top universities. They knew how to encourage Richard's intellectual and artistic interests, but they also understood the need for balance. Richard's father took him to baseball games, and, for Richard, that began a lifelong love of the game.

When Richard was 13 years old, he became a volunteer at the Children's Museum in Boston, which had a computer hooked up to a terminal in Cambridge, Massachusetts. The computer ran a language called Logo. Richard recalls, "I used to hack around with it. This was before 'hack' meant evil people breaking into things. Hacking was just having fun exploring the possibilities of the system. I wrote some programs that the visitors to the museum could play with. One of the programs was a simple game that allowed the user to think of a number and the computer would try to guess it."

At school, Richard studied advanced math and really enjoyed it. The one exception was differential equations. He says, "There are a zillion different kinds of differential equations, and to this day I have never felt the need to solve one in real life. So, I wasn't motivated to learn how. Probability was the opposite—most people found it hard, but I loved it because I saw the real-world applications like playing poker and counting cards at blackjack."

But even the classes at Harvard could not keep Richard interested. He says, "I'm sort of a dilettante. I've sampled lots of different things. I'd get just enough into them to the point that they ceased to be fascinating and I'd move onto something else."

After two years at Harvard, Richard left. He says, "I left to go out and make my fortune in Silicon Valley. I went out there, and after applying at about thirty companies, a receptionist who saw I didn't have a degree laughed at me. This nineteen-year-old girl was there looking at my application, and she said, 'You know, you're competing with people who have college degrees.' So I left disappointed. That company was Apple Computer."

But someone who was to become Richard's greatest mentor in the computer business hired him in 1979. This man understood that not all programmers of the future were going to have degrees. Richard smiles and says, with a twinkle in his eyes, "He asked me some programming questions and he liked the way I answered them. He was at Xerox PARC [Palo Alto Research Center] in Menlo Park, California, which, at the time, was probably the most prestigious place doing computer stuff. His name is Charles Simonyi." Simonyi has taken his place among the legendary programmers of our time. He knew what Richard Brodie could offer to the computer world.

Richard feels very fortunate to have worked for and with someone as brilliant as Charles Simonyi. "For someone as undisciplined as I am," says Richard, "having Charles as a coach was very effective. People attribute being hard core to Bill Gates, but I think Charles is more hard core than Bill ever was. Charles is so focused on results you couldn't help but be infected by his enthusiasm." One project at the time was called Smalltalk, and it had windows, icons, menus, and other properties later associated with Macs and Windows. Richard likes to imitate Charles's thick Hungarian accent. "Charles would say, 'Come on guys! The window of opportunity is closing. We gotta come out. We gotta be the first one!' There was a fire in people's bellies because Charles could paint an amazing picture of what we could do. We'd waste no time—we'd just get down and do it," says Richard. At Xerox, and later at Microsoft, Charles wanted Richard to work on the projects personally—to write the code. He saw Richard as a fine craftsman and artist. Richard took that as quite a compliment from someone like Charles.

At Xerox PARC, Charles and Richard began a lifelong friendship and working relationship. Richard points out how close they were, how similarly their minds worked. "Charles and I practically shared our brains. The communication between us was incredible." He recalls one project at Xerox called Bravo, where they worked together to develop a modeless word processor that had a graphical user interface. "In order to enter a word onto a document while working on the PCs of the time you would have to put the word processor into 'insert mode' before typing the word." Richard explains why this was such a hassle. "You'd forget what mode you were in. There was a rule of thumb called 'the cup of coffee test.' You had to be able to go get a cup of coffee in the middle of your work, and when you returned to your computer, you should not have to remember what mode you were in. If you were in some 'mode' and forgot to hit the escape key, what you typed might be interpreted as a command." This problem showed up with Microsoft's Multiplan version 1.0. Richard describes what happened. "If you were in command mode rather than 'alpha,' or typing mode, and you typed the word, 'today,' Multiplan would interpret that as a 'Transfer Options Delete All Yes' and poof! All your files were deleted. Bad stuff." He and Charles eventually solved the problem.

Xerox PARC's purpose was research. When that research was finished, the company would decide whether to patent or sell their products. It became increasingly obvious to Richard that Xerox was not about to take practical advantage of its research. He says, "Although Xerox PARC was about pure research, if you ask me, in practice they were on the one-yard line, ready to score the winning touchdown. They gave up. Charles used to say about Xerox's upper management, 'If they had owned the property at Sutters Mill, they would have ignored the yellow stuff and put up condominiums.' " Richard pauses to laugh. "The company decided they weren't getting enough revenue from Xerox PARC." Although Xerox PARC focused on research, even research companies are accountable for profit and loss.

Life at Microsoft

Richard joined Charles Simonyi at Microsoft in 1981—supposedly for just one summer. Richard relates the story in Charles's thick Hungarian accent. "Charles told Bill [Gates] that he wasn't going to try and get me to stay longer. He knew I had wanted to return to Harvard while we were at Xerox. Charles always felt bad for talking me out of it. He thought Xerox was a once-in-a-lifetime opportunity. But Bill said, 'Charles, what is the point in hiring this guy, and how much can he do in one summer?' Charles replied, 'If I had only fifty cents and I want to buy gold, do not tell me I cannot buy gold for fifty cents—tell me I can only buy fifty cents' worth of gold.'" Richard pauses to laugh. "I was the first and only guy Charles hired away from Xerox." But Richard would stay at Microsoft far longer than one summer, and he would become a legend in his own right.

Richard's first interview was with Steve Ballmer. Although Charles had highly recommended Richard, Microsoft has always been intensely cautious about hiring. Richard says, "Steve Ballmer knew as much about computer programming as I know about yacht racing. Still, he knew people very well. He had a trick—he would always ask programmers about hash tables." *Hash tables* are a computer science trick for looking things up in a table. They are a highly efficient mathematical tool that stores and processes index numbers in the computer. Richard told Steve about hash tables. "He didn't know much about them, but he knew when an answer was good or not. I guess when I answered him he liked what he heard," says Richard.

Soon after Richard started at Microsoft, he and Steve Ballmer went out for lunch at a little deli in Bellevue called Trebor's. Richard chuckles and says, "I mentioned that "Trebor" was "Robert" spelled backwards. Ballmer was just blown away. I mean, he was impressed. I really think it reinforced his estimation of me." Richard didn't mention that when he and his brother were boys, they spelled their names backward and used them to sign up for junk mail.

The first thing Richard did after he was hired was to go to Bill Gates's office and talk to him. "Bill was very impressive. He was this cheerful, smart young guy. I was twenty-one years old then and Bill was twenty-five. Bill showed me some source code for BASIC and said, 'You see these macros in here? We have those in so we can use the same source code for a number of different environments. We just turn on the assembler directives and tell it which platform it's being assembled for.' " Then Bill asked Richard something he'll never forget. "He asked me, 'Do you think that's a good idea?' It wasn't that he was testing me," Richard says. "He really wanted to know if I thought this was a good idea. I told him it might be a good idea depending on the circumstances—if all the versions were fairly similar and there were only small differences, then it was a good idea. But if there are a lot of differences you can end up making it very difficult to maintain. A change in one version has to be tested in all the versions." Richard saw that the issue was not clearcut, and the question about sharing source code persists at Microsoft to this day.

When Richard joined, he wasn't given a formal title. Richard was a programmer. Being a programmer at Microsoft was enough of a title, as it was considered a programmers' company. The first thing Richard did was to write the compiler Microsoft planned to use to make its new family of applications (now known as Microsoft Office) run on a variety of brands that were competing for dominance of the emerging microcomputer market. As with BASIC, Charles and Bill wanted to have one version of source code that would run on a number of platforms. The source code would compile into a pseudo-machine (p-code) rather than the machine code from the real machine. An interpreter would be written and would execute the p-code. "A lot of people thought that the PC business was going to be a long, hard-fought competition among many, many manufacturers like the Apple II, Tandy Radio Shack TRS-80, the Commodore, and the IBM, which was still secret at that point. We were going to have what Charles fondly referred to as 'the Revenue Bomb,' " Richard notes. "Along one axis, we would have a number of different products—MultiPlan, a word processor, a database, or whatever. On the other axis we would have different platforms like Apple, Radio Shack, and IBM. In that rectangular area described by the product of the number of new platforms and the number of the products would be the revenue. Unfortunately, while p-code made development *easier* it also made the program run *slower*." When Lotus 1-2-3 came along, it was faster than Multiplan. "It took us awhile to recover from that," Richard notes. P-code was a good and well-executed plan, but it was made irrelevant by the change in the market. One of Microsoft's strengths was the ability to absorb blows delivered by changing markets and continue to move forward.

Richard is best known for writing the first version of Microsoft Word. In the summer of 1982, he began work, and the final product was finished in October 1983. His mission was to write a program for a low-end word processor that used the same interface as Multiplan. With good humor, Richard recalls, "They told me it was designed to be a kind of flagship product of our series of Multiplan tools. They told me there had been some spec work done on it previously, but I kind of threw that away and just wrote what I wanted it to do." Version 1.0 actually had some very sophisticated features. For example, version 1.0 supported laser printers even thought they were not yet out. Richard says, "We knew they were coming out. We had proportional fonts and we had the ability to use measurements that were very fine. I invented the word 'twip,' which stands for a twentieth of a point. A point is a printer's unit of measure and it's approximately 1/72 of an inch. 'Twip' is still with us. It's used all over Windows." Users would not know about twips, but those who write Windows applications know about it. Richard also invented the term *combo box*. "I'm sure I was one of many to come up with the obvious idea of combining a list box and a text box. We used it in a prototype of Word for Windows."

Richard did not find Word a difficult project. "I had pretty much a free hand," he says. "It was a pretty small program, and I was familiar with word processing from my work at Xerox PARC with Charles."

Word version 1.0 was 80 percent Richard's code. The code was broken up into different files so that more than one person could work on it. Then it was merged together. Richard liked working alone or with just a few other programmers. He says, "I definitely existed in the era of the small programming group. Right now, that era still exists for the World Wide Web development. But for big programs like Word you now have about 100 people working on it because it's so complicated. That just gives me a headache—I *hate* that."

With Word, the basic algorithms had been written many times. The ideas stemmed from research done at Xerox PARC. Richard points out how different things were in the industry at that time: "This was back in the days before software patents, so nobody claimed these basic algorithms. At that time, it was considered purely a scientific endeavor."

Richard's moment of truth came when he finally showed Word to Bill Gates. Bill checked it out. Then he sent Richard an e-mail with a list of 17 deficiencies in the product. Richard remembers the day well. "I was called to action—I was on fire. I'd been working on this thing for a year and it still had all these things wrong with it. I stayed at Microsoft all weekend and tried to fix them. I think I fixed eleven of them. Most of the problems had to do with speed—too long to display, too long to save, and so on." Richard went on to explain that Word was supposed to run on a computer with one floppy disk and no hard disk. The IBM PC and the Apple II were the two chief target machines. To save something, the user would have to remove the floppy disk with the program. For example, if you used BASIC for doing your accounting, the program had to be small enough so it could be used in memory and could write out your program on the other disk. Then you'd stick the disk back in. "What a *nightmare!*" says Richard. After working through the weekend, Richard informed Bill of the status of the deficiencies by e-mail and sent him a new disk. Richard pauses and says, "When I saw him, Bill said, 'I can't believe you fixed all those things. That's incredible!' I said, 'Well, you sent me the list of things.' And Bill said, 'I know, but I send that to everyone. Nobody's ever done anything about it before.'" Laughing at the memory, Richard says, "I didn't know any better. I didn't know I was *not* supposed to be able to fix them!"

Richard laughs and recalls, "One thing that just blew Bill away was an optimization of the display speed. We actually formatted as you typed. Every time you inserted one character, the screen would update to show exactly what was going to be printed. Initially, that was slow, which is probably why no one else had it. I thought hard about it. The slowness was caused by the processor mostly rewriting characters that were already on the display. To minimize the slowness, I made the program to be very clever and only change characters that needed to be changed."

For most users of Microsoft products, the mouse is an important tool. But it was almost left out of the scheme of things until Richard came to its rescue. Jeff Raikes joined Microsoft as a marketing manager about the time Richard was finishing Word. He asked Richard how they could shave some time off of the shipping schedule. Richard says, "I was always a realist when it came to schedules, and I was known as an anomaly in the industry because my products actually shipped on time. When people would come in and ask for new features, even little ones, I would ask them if it was okay to slip the schedule half a week or a week. They would be very frustrated, but where did they think the time was going to come from? They seemed to think we could just sneak in a feature without it taking any time."

Raikes wanted to move the schedule up because he wanted to coordinate the launch of Word with a large media promotion and get it out in time for Christmas. He asked Richard for a detailed list of all the remaining work items: mouse support, tabs, integration of the printing code, as well as other tasks. Richard recalls the incident. "Jeff looked at what needed to be done and of course the thing that jumped out at him was what we called mouse support. None of our competitors had it, and he thought it would be okay to cut because of that. I didn't agree because I had seen how much easier it was to work with a mouse while I was at Xerox. So I promised to work long hours and put in mouse support in one week. Jeff looked at me skeptically and asked if I could really do it in one week. I went through my mental map of how I was planning to do it and I told him a week was realistic. I started working on a Sunday and actually handed Jeff a disk on Wednesday at lunchtime."

Richard was always adamant about shipping on time. Word was shipped on schedule.

At that time, in 1983, reviewers covering the PC scene thought Word was a great product, but they all doubted the future of the mouse. Until then, all PC software responded to keyboard commands, and it took a while for people to embrace the new tool. Ironically, Microsoft has become famous for its mouse support products. Although Richard had no way of knowing it at the time, one of his key achievements at Microsoft was single-handedly saving mouse software support.

Richard likes to talk about the world of programming, which has its own traditions and customs. Most programmers make what are known as "comments" in their source code. By accessing these comments, another programmer who wants to go in and change things can determine what the original programmer intended in the source code.

Another thing programmers get a kick out of doing is writing "Easter eggs," or hidden treasures, in their programs. They're usually a way of getting the names of the development team into the program, but they take other forms as well. Of course, most programmers try to find these hidden treasures. According to Richard, Excel '98 has a Quake-like mini–video game in it. Easter eggs are pretty much a programming world secret. The average user would not have any idea how to find them, even if he or she knew they were in the software.

As a top-notch programmer, Richard would write the code from the top down. He explains why he believes it's the best way to write. "You get the big picture, and then you fill in the details. They teach that in college. But sometimes I'd get down to one of the low-level routines and realize it wasn't going to work. I'd have to go back and start all over again. I'd do that because there would be an architectural flaw in a program if I didn't. For the user, flaws could be very frustrating. Things would not work smoothly. Most of the time, functions would work properly, but once in a while they would not." For example, a later version of Word, written by many programmers, has a problem with the spell checker. Sometimes it will not accept the command to proof in English, leaving the user without the spell-checker function.

Richard says, "One of the great things we had in Word 1.0 was 'undo.' This was a real advanced feature for personal computers. 'Undo' was very hard. There were so many different things you could do that it was almost impossible to figure out how to undo each of them. We really had to think about what it meant. What does it mean when you delete some text and type in some new text? What does undoing mean? I thought undoing meant you went back to the original text. You don't just leave it deleted. We made a lot of decisions like that. Overall, 'undo' became a feature that became a 'must have.' "

Richard understands what makes a great programmer as opposed to a good programmer. He says, "You have to have certain psychological drives. One is for efficiency. A good programmer is extremely parsimonious. He will not have one extra line of code. It won't feel right if you have it. Another is flexibility—you have to constantly be able to turn things around in your mind and look at them from different angles. The third thing you need is an intensely critical nature. You have to be able to take a complex structure and find the flaws in it, relentlessly. Without those things, you're not going to be able to produce great code."

According to Richard, programming is a creative endeavor. It is not just applied science. As a programmer, Richard is able to picture the entire program in his head. "Without that ability," he says, "you're lost. You have to be very good at visualizing complex systems. I think certain skills can be learned, but it seems to me that the best programmers are just born that way. It's an innate talent." If one tiny part of a program didn't work, Richard would scrap everything and start over again. Not all programmers will do this. He clarifies the creative aspect of writing code when he relates the following anecdote: "When my father took me to see the play about Mozart, *Amadeus,* the thing that sticks most in my mind is that Mozart could write a piece down, never changing a note, from start to finish. Isaac Asimov, the writer, did that too. That always astounded me. Although I had the capacity to picture the whole system, I'd still go back and rewrite and redesign. I want my programs to be perfect so that they work well for the end user."

Richard also implemented the mail-merge feature in Word 1.1. After that, he designed user interfaces for new features such as document types, spelling check, and tables. Richard laughs and says, "I actually designed that squiggly red line for Word for Windows 1.0, but I forgot to tell anyone how to implement it before I left the company to return to Harvard. When I came back to work on Access, I ran into Chris Mason, who was the development manager for Word. Chris thought that feature was too hard. In thirty seconds I explained to Chris how to do it and he instantly understood. The next thing I know, there is a new version of Word with that squiggly red underline as it spell-checked in the background. I was so happy. It's one of my favorite features!"

In 1983, during Christmas, Richard was on vacation in a remote part of Puerto Rico. He had just shipped Word and would return to Harvard in a few weeks. "Bill got the phone number of my girlfriend in Puerto Rico and told her that I could expect an offer from him to be his personal assistant. The days went by, but there was no phone call from Bill. The day before I was scheduled to return to Harvard, I called and spoke to Jo Ann Rahal, head of personnel. She said she'd find out about the offer. She called back and told me they were FedExing me the offer. I thought, 'Cool!' When the package arrived, I read the letter from Bill over and over again. It was a very important position, and I would be involved in every technical aspect of the company. I could have another job in six months if I still wanted to finish school, but Bill could not guarantee it would be this job. I bit."

Richard laughs and says, "But I didn't know what my responsibilities were as Bill's assistant." It was very hard for Richard. "He really goes through assistants, let me tell you. Mostly because he's so busy. You have to be extremely self-directed, which I am not. I loved Bill, but I *hated* that job. I didn't know what I was supposed to do. It was very frustrating." While acting as Bill's assistant, Richard and others designed Word for Windows, a project that was code-named Cashmere. Of Cashmere, Richard says, "It was actually supposed to be like Windows 95. I think we bit off a little more than we could chew at that point. Bill wanted a program that did absolutely everything with words and data. I was happy just getting a great window word processor out. And, as is usual in such cases, we ended up with neither." Richard also worked on the standard Microsoft user interface and put in touches that are still seen today.

Richard and Bill rarely came in to work at the same time. When they were in the office together, Richard often ended up frustrated. "I hardly ever saw him," says Richard. "He'd have me working on one thing, researching something, and speccing something, and then he'd come in and say, 'I'd better find out how hard it would be to put Lotus 1-2-3 user interface on top of Word,' or something like that." Richard would go to work on it and then Bill would tell him they didn't need it anymore. Bill was very busy running the company. But for all of his frustration, Richard admired Bill. "Mostly, it was an honor to be there absorbing all that stuff going on. I just really enjoyed Bill's company. He's a very interesting and charming guy."

Richard says he holds the record for leaving and returning to the company. "I left five or six times," he says. During one of his "returns," Richard worked on Access. It drove him crazy. He recalls, "After I had optimized the disk access to be superfast, we kept running into some very weird errors. They would happen only once in awhile, when we were running on a disk drive on another machine on the network, and only when we were doing superefficient big disk operations. If you ran the debugger and stepped through the code one instruction at a time, it didn't happen! Truly a programmers' nightmare." Richard was convinced that the bug was in the operating system. The operating systems people were convinced it was in Richard's code. It turned out to be a bug in some hand-written machine code at a very low level of the operating system. Richard says, "The problem was fixed and they hustled the new code over to manufacturing."

The working environment at Microsoft had changed a great deal during the 13 years since Richard had joined it, and he had become increasingly frustrated. "After the company went public in 1986, it occurred to me that I wasn't happy and I was never going to be happy there. There was only one job at Microsoft that I thought was a really good job and Bill already had that one." Richard laughs. "I really never felt like part of the inner circle there, even when I was Bill's assistant. I really like to be a big fish, even if it's a small pond. It may be a personality flaw in me, but there it is." Richard realizes that Bill has been very generous and understanding. "We never do anything to hurt the relationship. In some ways, a working relationship that is close is like a marriage. It can be difficult unless you keep a clear head. But Bill and I are both very rational, and I consider him a friend."

In January 1994, Richard left Microsoft. He has not returned. But Bill said to him, "The door is always open." Richard says, "Microsoft is not for everyone. You have to be pretty thick-skinned. I've seen people get chewed up and spit out by Microsoft. I look at it this way: In the old days you had fairy tales in which the prince would go out to make his fortune. He would sail away to foreign lands, fight armies, make a fortune and bring it back, and marry the princess. I look on Microsoft in the same way—a place where a young man could go out and make his fortune. A young man tends to be more interested in that kind of a lifestyle. It's not a place where you'll have warm fuzzies, although there's certainly some enjoyment and adventure there. You can see why so many people are retiring—it's a place you want to retire *from*. It's very fast paced and hard core. If that's what you're looking for at a particular time in your life, then it's wonderful and fun."

The bigger Microsoft became, the more disillusioned Richard felt: "I finally 'got it' that the people who ran the world were not workers, no matter how smart or effective they were. Workers are in the service of the promoters and capitalists. It made me kind of sad. We tend to have this myth that if we work hard and diligently we can rise to the top." But that knowledge also motivated Richard to go out and learn social and communication skills that make people leaders in our society. He says, "It took me ten years to get to where I can even glimpse what techniques the great communicators and manipulators use to achieve huge things. That search prompted me to write two books: *Getting Past OK,* about that particular personal growth experience, and *Virus of the Mind,* about how it is that most of us are the unwitting receptors of other people's ideas and mental programming. So, in the end, the learning experience was worth going through that disillusionment."

Having brains can bring as many curses as rewards. Richard muses, "Looking back, one thing I think is kind of sad is how little emotional reward there is for being smart. It doesn't win friends, get girls, or really even get the approval of adults except the rare generous intellectual. I always thought they should give out varsity letter jackets for chess and math teams. I mean, what are we rewarding? Kids who are willing and big enough to go out on a football field and break each other's bones?" As with so many smart people, intellectual development for Richard came at the expense of social and emotional development. He has spent the last 8 to 10 years working on his social development. He says, "At thirty-eight, I'm just now catching up to the point where I'm not a complete nerd.

"When I joined Microsoft, I had no inkling that it would be so successful. How could I? It's really hard to get your mind around it. When Romulus and Remus came to Rome, did they have any sense that there was going to be a Holy Roman Empire? I was just happy thinking my software was going to be in a box in a store somewhere. I think Charles had an idea of it though." Charles Simonyi built the applications for Multiplan, Word, Chart, and Excel that are now a billion-dollar business. "Charles is a good motivator and he's technically brilliant. You can say the same thing about Bill. The thing about Bill is, he has a sense for the *game*. Everything is a poker game to him. He has this incredible mind for probabilities and bets and payoffs. He makes every bet that he thinks has a good payoff. He's actually quite playful."

It is hard to predict whether Richard Brodie will ever return to Microsoft. He says, "In the early days it was fun. I was immersed in creating a product that was going to make such an impact on the world. That's very motivating. But now, programming gives me a headache!"

Life after Microsoft

Since retiring in 1994, Richard Brodie has spent much of his time writing about subjects that have concerned him for years. The thesis of *Getting Past OK* is that you can reprogram your mind so that it is united with your purpose in life. In *Virus of the Mind,* which was mentioned on *Oprah,* Richard explores "memes" or mental programmings that affect our minds much like a computer virus. Richard's concern is that manipulative people are starting to create all kinds of "designer mind viruses" to gain power, money, sex—anything. Advertising, religious cults, and institutions can program your mind through repetition and by playing on your insecurity and spiritual yearning. He believes it is a truly new phenomenon that is changing the face of our culture. The books were published by Integral Press, Richard's publishing house. He also has a web page dedicated to memes, called Memes Central. He is currently working on a novel. For Richard, writing books is much like writing code for software programs. It is creative and challenging.

Brodie Technology Group is another of Richard's companies. The company does software consulting for

Microsoft and smaller companies. Richard is the CEO and only employee. He also sees himself becoming a computer programmer's agent, much like a sports or literary agent.

When questioned about any downsides of success and wealth, Richard merely laughs. He feels that the only problem might be the lack of motivation—no wolf at the door. Mainly, Richard sees a lot of young men and women who have been empowered by wealth to take the path of self-discovery and find themselves. He admires Scott Oki and Ida Cole for their philanthropy. He also admires others who have risked all to start their own companies. He says, "Me? I've taken being a dilettante to levels of greatness!"

RUSSELL BORLAND

"The Author"

■

Microsoft: 1980–1997

Master Technical Writer and Head Writer,
Microsoft Press International

RUSSELL BORLAND

"The Author"

Russell Borland wears his graying hair in a braid. He dresses in jeans and a sweatshirt. His casual appearance camouflages his various talents and interests. He has a Ph.D. in English literature, is a Harley-Davidson enthusiast, and writes best-sellers.

In 1980, Russell was hired as the technical writer for Microsoft. Russell wrote manuals for BASIC, FORTRAN, Macro Assembler, RAMCard, and other languages.

In 1984, Bill Gates asked Russell to join the team working on Word for Windows version 1. In 1988, Russell transferred to Microsoft Press. His idea was to write a book, which became *Working with Word for Windows*. The rest is history. Russell's books have been best-sellers throughout the world. Among his 17 books are *Running Microsoft Word for Windows*, *Microsoft WordBasic Primer*, and *Microsoft Exchange in Business*.

Because of Russell's achievements at Microsoft, users around the world can easily use and understand Microsoft's software programs. When Russell retired in 1997, only Bill Gates and Steve Ballmer had worked at Microsoft longer.

The Path to Microsoft

When Russell Borland was in high school in West Linn, Oregon, he thought that one day he would become a physicist or a mathematician. He liked those subjects and did very well in them. However, he took all the accelerated classes the school had to offer. He credits one of those—an English class—for his writing ability. Russell says, "We had to write all the time—it was just something we were required to do. One class taught us how to take the advanced placement tests. Part of that class was about getting organized. And we had to diagram sentences, which is both useless and powerful at the same time. You got a sense of the structure of a sentence. Much of that is gone in education now."

Russell continued his education at Whitworth College in Spokane, Washington. He found math boring, and recalls, "It was a liberal arts college so I had to major in something. The strongest department was English, so I decided to take advantage of that." A class in literary criticism taught Russell how to write concisely and clearly. He recalls, "The rule was, we could only use two pages to write about a story. The paragraphs had to look like pictures. We'd take a story like Faulkner's 'The Bear' and try to say something intelligent and complete in two pages. I'd write a lot of pages and then condense it—get rid of the fluff." In 1968, Russell earned a bachelor of arts degree in English.

After serving in the Army, in 1973 Russell earned a master of arts degree from Portland State. His master's thesis examined Thomas Hardy's seven major novels. Russell says, "The crux of the paper was that the characters have the ability to exert their will to achieve a state of grace, but they *don't*. They let their emotions get in the way of everything and they destroy themselves." Apropos of his thesis, Russell observes, "There are some people who just won't do what they need to do. Lots of people are whiners. So many people say, 'It's not my fault; it's the other person.'" Unbeknownst to Russell at the time, he would find this philosophy of will and accomplishment a good fit with a company called Microsoft.

Russell continued his studies at the University of Washington, and in 1979 he earned a Ph.D. in English. He wanted to teach at the college/university level. But jobs were tough to come by because many schools at that time were under pressure to hire minorities, and there were few teaching jobs for a white, middle-class males in 1979. "I turned to computer writing," says Russell. The same year, he joined Seafirst Bank in Seattle, writing procedures for its central office. He used Seafirst's in-house self-study program to learn more about computers. The written procedures helped employees get data ready to enter into the computer and also helped them read the reports after they were output. Russell recalls, "The division, in its wisdom, decided that my group was no longer necessary." He had until the end of the year to find another job.

Like most people who search for a job, Russell looked at ads in the newspapers. He asked himself what he wanted to do. He concluded that he would like to write manuals for a software company. Russell says, "One day I saw an ad in the paper for a technical writer. It wasn't any more specific than that except for mentioning computer documentation." Russell made the phone call—it was to an agency. He described his experience and sent in his resume.

One week later, Russell received a call from a company called Microsoft. Russell laughs and says, "I had never heard of Microsoft." Russell interviewed with Andrea Lewis, the head of Technical Publications, and three days later they talked again. Andrea wanted Russell to talk with Paul Allen. Russell smiles and says, "Toward the end of my interview with Paul, he asked if I had any questions. I knew that I should have kept my mouth shut, but instead I blurted out, 'Everyone I talk to about Microsoft mentions how young you and Bill are.' Paul stared at me for about thirty seconds without saying anything. I sat there thinking, 'Oh, f–! I just blew it!' Then Paul threw back his head and roared with laughter." Paul then explained to Russell what he and Bill had already accomplished in the few years Microsoft had been doing business. Two days later Microsoft offered Russell the job.

Life at Microsoft

Russell began work for Microsoft in July 1980. Management told him what the company did. "They gave me an outline of the products, but what you have to understand is that this was before MS-DOS." At the time, the company had programming languages such as BASIC, BASIC Compiler, FORTRAN, COBOL, and Assembler. Microsoft had a few game products such as Olympic Decathlon and Adventure for the TRS-80 Radio Shack machine. It also had Typing Tutor for the TRS-80 and SoftCard, which was developed by Paul Allen for the Apple II. Russell leans back and says, "The story related to me was that Bill said back then, 'BASIC we eat, everything else we smoke.' That meant that BASIC was really the funding for the company until MS-DOS came along."

When Russell joined Microsoft, it had fewer than 40 employees. He found the work environment to be extremely casual: "People worked all kinds of strange hours. There were people who came in at dark and left at dawn. If people couldn't sleep, they'd come in at three in the morning. There was an employee no longer with the company who used the men's rest room as his personal shower facility. Mind you, there weren't any shower stalls in the rest room. He simply hooked up a sprayer hose to a faucet and showered. The building management was constantly complaining about someone using the rest room to take showers."

Even in 1980, most people had their own offices. On the day Russell started work, Andrea Lewis took him on a tour of the computer room. Russell says, "Marc McDonald and I think Steve Woods were setting up the second seventy-megabyte hard disk drive for their DEC1010, which everybody used. It was a time-share minicomputer. So the total capacity of the thing went up to about a hundred and forty megabytes of hard disk drive storage. You look at what's on people's desks now and the equipment is so fast and powerful. But that's the way it was then." He belonged to a department called Technical Publications. "We did all the manuals for the products. It was just me and my boss, Andrea Lewis. She did brochures, PR releases, and advertising," he says.

Microsoft had a Wang word processor that had just a few terminal links. The company didn't use it very often, as most of the files were stored on a DEC1010. "We printed manuals on a line printer; we'd just put in eight-and-a-half-inch-wide unlined fanfold and we printed out the pages. For OEM licensing customers we used to copy the documentation files onto tape—like the big tapes you see in old movies about mainframe computers. It was interesting because we could run any of the programming languages right on the computer as we were writing about them." Russell's recollections of just two decades ago show how astonishingly fast the computer industry has advanced.

One day early in his career Russell recalls telling Andrea, "As far as I can see, there's not going to be much work in the future." Andrea said "Whoa!" and pulled out a list of six upcoming projects. Russell says, "So we just kept going. Then MS-DOS changed everything. After that, the applications came and changed everything once again." The vision statement for the company was much the same then as it is now. "Microsoft wanted to develop the software that will make it possible for every home to have a computer on every desktop."

While he worked at Microsoft, Russell encountered no bureaucracy. He says, "It was a flat company. There was Bill and Paul and everybody else. Steve Ballmer was sort of in between. I reported to Andrea and Andrea reported to Bill. There weren't many memos. Microsoft was not big on memos. Communication was mostly spoken. At that time, we didn't even have e-mail." Later, as Microsoft Press grew, it was still out of the corporate mainstream. Russell says, "Elton Welke [the publisher at Press] seemed to work pretty hard at handling the relationship between Press and the executive officers of Microsoft. We weren't dragged into it that much. Press seemed more like an independent publisher than simply another division of Microsoft."

Microsoft already had a reputation for being volatile, but Russell usually took that part of the corporate culture in his stride. "Up until the late 1980s, there was a strong confrontational style at the company," Russell remembers. "If someone yelled at you, you yelled back. I'm not that kind of person. My strategy was to go silent and let whomever was yelling rant on. I drove those yelling types crazy. They wanted combat. When there wasn't any combativeness they got frustrated. As long as someone was yelling back they had a hope of overpowering the opposition. When the opponent is silent and stubborn they have no hope. They don't know what to do. Times like that were aggravating, but kind of fun, too."

The late 1980s would replace this confrontational style with the idea of teamwork. Russell notes, "Microsoft later got infected with the management bug that sees any disagreement as not being 'a team player.' This was not universally true, and on important issues it was still possible to disagree and propose alternatives. But in many ways, this standard management ploy became gospel."

But Russell liked his job too much to let minor aggravations get in his way. He remembers that after he had been with the company for three months, he knew he had found a home for his talents. Russell enjoyed writing manuals. "I knew that this was where I wanted to be." The casual environment aided Russell in his work. "We were on our own," he points out. "Each individual contributor was expected to do many things. Your creativity and problem solving was accepted. They let you give free rein to your creativity, for the most part."

By the spring of 1982, Microsoft had about nine technical writers. Russell became the manager of the technical writers group, which wrote documentation for the programs. That job lasted one year. When Andrea Lewis left the company she asked Russell if he wanted to become manager of Technical Publications. Technical writers write the documentation for the programs; the production editors were responsible for publishing the manuals. Russell says, "I decided that I did. That lasted about a year, and then I decided I didn't want to do that. I wasn't very good at it. When I started, there were nineteen people. A year later, there were fifty-five people and about a dozen temporaries. You can manage nineteen people sort of by the seat of your pants. Seventy people takes real organization and management skills." Russell spent 50 percent of his day on e-mail. A third of his day was spent listening to five supervisors and dealing with people problems. Russell laughs and says, "That left about one-sixth of the day to think of ways to guide the department. By that time, I didn't have much energy left. I always felt like I was behind about three or four eight balls."

By 1984, Russell had had enough of managing people. He sums up his thoughts on the subject. "At times I felt the job was like baby-sitting. One employee came into my office to complain about the software developers on a project. While the litany of complaints rolled out, I kept thinking, 'I have to go through this at home with my teenage sons. I don't need this at work, too.' The complaints always ended with a question to me, 'What are you going to do about it?' " Russell really disliked political and social maneuvering as well as confrontation.

In 1984, Russell was given a choice between remaining a manager or becoming an active contributor to a project. Russell opted for the latter. He was offered the position as a writer for a project called Cashmere. "There was supposed to be an individual group made up of all the people necessary for a product: programmers, program managers, product managers, writers, and testers. Bill wanted Cashmere done in *one year,* starting September 1984! The concept of Cashmere was close to Microsoft Office, but not as powerful," says Russell. It had a flat file manager rather than a relational database. It was supposed to have e-mail as Office now has. "The more we got into it," Russell states, "the more we realized that this was a huge thing to try and put together. To do it in one year was totally impossible given the state of the technology." The project bumbled along, and Russell thought that the leader of the project was not a very good manager. He says, "The whole thing just sort of fell apart. Part of it was turf wars and part of it was the lack of leadership. Windows was not yet developed far enough to support the kinds of things this product was supposed to do." But all was not lost. Russell concludes, "The project was restarted and became Word for Windows."

From September 1984 until April 1988, Russell worked on documentation for Word for Windows 1.0. "We had done Word for the Macintosh, so it became a matter of adapting Word for Macintosh for Windows," Russell points out. Word for Windows was a porting of Word for Macintosh 3.0. It had the same feature set and program organization. Russell was one of five people who worked on the design of the program. He says, "We'd been assigned new programmers and we'd hash out the features. After that, I was supposed to write the manuals. I informally headed up the team of people who were also working on the manual and the CBT [computer-based training] group."

After Russell wrote the manuals, they went into editing, testing, and production. When he was no longer involved with the project, he contacted Microsoft Press and said, "I know all of this stuff about Word. I'd hate to have it just disappear. Would you be interested in having me author a book about Word with Microsoft Press?" Press was very interested. Min Yee, the creative maverick and publisher at Microsoft Press, gave the go-ahead.

A new era at Microsoft Press was about to begin thanks to Russell's foresight and dedication. His first and subsequent books would put Microsoft Press on the publishing world map. Originally, Press was founded to garner free publicity. Russell explains the evolution of Press. "It had been just a fancy PR entity that was costing Microsoft money. The first step was to turn it into something that would sustain itself. Once it got to the point of making money, which the company liked, the emphasis changed. They had discovered over the years that the name 'Microsoft' was actually a drawback. People thought Press was a vanity publisher for Microsoft or that Microsoft was just dumping into Press the documentation they should have been supplying for free. But within about two years, the name was no longer that negative and consumers realized no one knew Microsoft products as well as their own people. At first, though, the name 'Microsoft' was downplayed on the cover of the books. On some covers it was so small you could hardly read it." After 1993, the company imprint was a prime selling point.

When Russell arrived at Microsoft Press, people were using a variety of machines. Russell says, "I was using a 286 to write manuscript. Others were using Macs for some artwork and some of the cover designs. The Press was using a dedicated typesetting system for typography. The word processing people were using an old version of Word." Russell laughs at the memory. "They were usually about one version behind what I was using. It was a strange kind of setup—everything was all hacked together. We tried to do things electronically, but it wasn't coordinated very well."

By 1988, there were about 50 people working at Press. It was difficult to ascertain the exact number, as Press used freelance proofreaders and indexers who were not actually working at an office inside Press. Russell muses, "It's ironic that I transferred to a part of the corporation that was the size of Microsoft when I first joined."

However, Russell did consider leaving Press and interviewed with another company. He explains, "At Microsoft, programmers were the top dogs in the food chain. At the other company, technical writers were the top dogs. But I had a chance to write a book at Press. I thought that I'd keep writing books and see how it turned out." Russell chuckles. "It kept me going for another nine years!"

Russell began work on the book, *Working with Word for Windows.* He says, "The books at the time were very different from manuals. There were almost no step-by-step procedures; everything was written out in paragraph form. There was real de-emphasis on any historical or sidebar material. There was an extreme emphasis on being as nontechnical as you could be. The idea was to explain very technical things in ways that were not technical. In addition, there was a sense that you did not have to cover every nook and cranny of a product. That was a relief. In a manual, everything had the same emphasis; every teeny tiny feature is equally important as the most amazing and widely used feature. It's like speaking in a monotone voice."

In writing *Word for Windows* and subsequent books, Russell's organizational skill served him quite well. "The first thing I always did was an outline," Russell says. "Probably the greatest strength I have as a writer is organization. With a piece of software, you might not know everything about the product when you start or when you get the outline done. It's hard to initially gauge the whole scope of the product or the huge number of features in a product and how they're connected. It changes." Some features would stay and others would go. Some features would be expanded. Russell explains, "You start out with a basic outline based on specifications, and pretty soon you're adding more sections, throwing some out, or changing and rearranging them. An outline will change since it's a reflection of the product.

"In a book of this kind," Russell says, "it is possible, to some extent, to let your voice come through. Manuals are meant to be absolutely anonymous. Nobody is identified with the manual—only the company is identified."

Russell received guidance from the people he worked with at Press. "I'd do a chapter, turn it in, and they'd make comments. I'd go back and revise it. But I'd always think about what would make a useful or interesting book. I'd look at books of instruction and directions for noncomputer or nontechnical things. I was always on the lookout for pictorial presentations of instructions and directions. That's how I learned to write the book," Russell says.

The work was hard, but gratifying, for Russell. He'd write about 200 pages a month, sometimes 300 pages when he worked on revisions. The first edition was called *Working with Word for Windows.* That title went through two editions: *WinWord 1.0* and *WinWord 1.1.* Beginning with version 2.0, *Working with Word for Windows* had become *Running Microsoft Word for Windows,* which sold very well over the years.

However, not all his books did well. *Word Basic Primer* and *Word for Windows 2.0 Macros* did not live up to expectations. The market was a small niche. Russell elaborates, "I had hoped that *Word Basic Primer,* in particular, would be for people who were just interested in using it as a glorified word processor. Maybe they'd want to do a few macros to make their life easier. Either they didn't know about the book or they didn't care." But *Getting Started with Windows 3.1* was a success. He says, "That one actually did pretty well and was in print for four years. That's a really long time for a software book."

Once in a while, Russell became frustrated at Press. "People at Press had tools in place, but there was no one to make them upgrade the tools. Some people were very reluctant to upgrade even though it would have made their lives a lot easier. They had their procedures and methods and were very comfortable with them. That didn't change for quite a while. It was just hard to believe that they weren't taking advantage of the newer products." Russell sighs, "It was really their problem. I just concentrated on writing the manuscripts."

At Microsoft Press, authors do not own the books—project editors own the books. Russell steeples his hands and says, "You beat your head against the wall if you go head-to-head with an editor. They usually have the last say anyway. You get to the point where you're sort of resigned. I would simply say to myself, 'I'm going to do the manuscript and do the best I can. And they're going to do what they want with it. That's the end of it.' "

Along the way, there were a few editors who really frustrated Russell. He says, "I got to the point where I didn't look at the marked-up manuscript. It was so frustrating to see how much wording they had changed. It strikes me as being a matter of style. They want to read it and write it this way and I want to read it and write it another way." Most of the time, editors did not give him a reason for the changes. Russell says, "They just did it. They used to give me the excuse that it was 'house style.' It really aggravated me because my view is, a style guide is simply default. If you have an ambiguous situation and things can be done in two ways, then it is done in house style. But you don't use it to force a manuscript into a vanilla shape. That's one of the ways you lose an author's voice."

Russell maintains that this is an old and ongoing problem for writers. He says, "If you think about it, most editors are frustrated writers. It's also not unusual for anybody who touches any kind of project to want to make their own contribution and to justify their existence. But it's not done maliciously. When people work together on any kind of a project they are going to have differing points of view."

Over the years, quiet lobbying began on behalf of Microsoft authors. The idea was to try to maintain the author's voice in the book. "The message has gotten through, and that part of writing the book has become better over the years."

While at Press, Russell worked with the larger-than-life publisher, Min Yee. Russell recalls some of the anecdotes that made Min a legend at Microsoft. "Min loved cars. While we were at Press together he owned a Mercedes, a Ferrari Testarossa, a Miata, and an Acura. When the Miatas first came out, Min was so eager to get one that he flew to Sacramento, bought it, and drove it home. He was well recognized for his speedy driving, even in the Microsoft parking lots."

Russell put in long hours at the company. But he is quick to qualify what that means. "People say the hours at Microsoft are horrendous. Most of the time, the hours are as bad as you want to make them. One joke at Microsoft was that 'flextime' meant you could work as many hours as you wanted over forty. You have to decide if you're using your time productively or just putting in time." Russell notes that many people appeared to be working very hard when they were really just spinning their wheels. "When I first started at Microsoft," says Russell, "I only worked eight hours a day. But I observed early on that programmers worked long hours, but this was their *hobby*. They enjoyed doing that more than anything else in the world. If they worked eight hours a day, what are they going to do when they go home? Work on their hobby? It's the same thing. In my entire career at Microsoft, no one has ever said to me that I should work more hours."

Enthusiasm for his work kept Russell going. He says, "If you're just fascinated with the stuff and all the new things that are happening and the new possibilities, then the time just takes care of itself."

On another aspect of the working environment, Russell observes, "Microsoft is based on merit, not politics or nepotism. If you do a good job and contribute, then you'll be rewarded. In some companies you have to be nice to the right person. Some bosses won't like you, or they might steal your idea. I was really glad that corporate politics was not a daily part of my work life. I found those aspects refreshing. I very much appreciated that. The only time politics caused me problems was when I managed people. That's why I didn't like it."

Despite the competition, Microsoft Press books are easily recognized and have sold very well. Russell does not take full credit for this. He says, "I think part of it is that it's Microsoft; people think we know our own products. Part of it is just the energy that Microsoft Press representatives have spent to get the books into the bookstores— to get the shelf space and some recognition. Microsoft Press prides itself, sometimes overly so, on making very high quality books. The author's contribution is part of it, too. The authors that Press works with produce good, quality manuscripts that can be made into good, quality books."

Russell felt that one of his greater achievements was rewriting *Word for the DOS* manual for version 2.0 in just three weeks at the same time he had to learn a new operating system (UNIX) and deal with a new editor (E) and a new formatter (T-ROFF). Another key achievement was writing the manuscripts for four large books in a single year: *Running Word 97, Running Outlook 97, Introducing Windows 98,* and *Word 97 Step by Step Advanced Topics.*

As Russell continued to succeed at Microsoft, his personal life suffered. In 1988, he and his wife separated, and in 1989 they divorced. "We had a fancy house on Lake Sammamish. I had a BMW and she had a Peugeot. We had fancy artifacts around the house. We were living a kind of quasi-snobbish, yuppie lifestyle. I got to the point where my lifestyle was a burden. I had possessions and I worried that they would be stolen. You can spend a lot of your time fretting about your possessions and your success." But Russell learned from that experience and downsized his lifestyle.

Today, Russell has strong advice for people. "Don't be a whiner," he cautions. "Do whatever you need to do to get where you want to go. While I was at Seafirst Bank and studying computers, I decided I wanted to write manuals for a small software company. I was willing to wait five years until I was prepared enough for one to find me attractive as a good hire. I didn't have to wait five years, but you need that kind of patience and willingness to do what it takes to get there. It's the kind of attitude you've got to have."

Russell decided to retire after 17 years with Microsoft. He would not trade his years there for anything. As a motorcycle enthusiast, he wanted more time to ride. It rained too much in Seattle. And Microsoft stock prices were up. It was time to move on. Russell laughs and says, "I didn't need more money. In the last year I wrote four books. Being over fifty years old, the pace was a bit too strong."

Life after Microsoft

Russell has come full circle and returned to a comfortable but simple lifestyle in the country near Ukiah, California. It is similar to the way in which he grew up in Oregon. He and his partner, Loretta, read, garden, and ride their Harleys around the country. He enjoys his retirement and takes a nap every day.

Currently, Russell is working on a novel. Occasionally, he teaches an Internet class on Word for Training Associates of Mesa, Arizona. The class is based on the Microsoft Press book, *Word 97 Step by Step, Complete Course.*

Neil Evans

"The Professor"

Microsoft: 1983–1994

Chief Information Officer

Member, Executive Staff

NEIL EVANS

"The Professor"

An avid jogger, Neil Evans is lean and lithe. His blond hair is cropped short. Although he is in his 40s, he has the agility and energy of a 20-year-old.

Neil moves and talks quickly, completely focused on the task at hand. He likes to get directly to the point. A man of many talents and enthusiasms, he is equally at home living in the wilderness, doing computer science, researching education technology, riding a Harley-Davidson, and making films.

Neil Evans is recognized as one of the nation's most successful chief information officers. In 1983, without a precedent to guide him, Neil founded and managed Microsoft's Information Technology Group, which then set up the company's internal worldwide network, MIS business systems, electronic mail, and database servers. Before Neil came on board, Microsoft International had no e-mail, nor did the company have an efficient way to manage its OEM (original equipment manufacturers) license agreements.

The Path to Microsoft

"When I was very young, I always thought I was going to be a professor," says Neil. As a young man growing up in Illinois, Neil saw the educational world as a haven for ideas and learning. In that world, he could share his thoughts and questions with young people. Summer jobs during high school in the sweltering Midwest reinforced his academic ambitions. "I've put shingle roofs on houses in August and worked in television factories when it was a hundred and twenty degrees inside. That gets you good and motivated," says Neil.

"My parents were kind of lower middle class; they didn't have a lot of money for me to go to a really good school," says Neil. But he found a way. As a resident of Illinois, he received a state scholarship and studied math, computer science, and philosophy at Northwestern University. Neil chose not to attend the University of Chicago. "It was a school for eggheads. I didn't want that," Neil recalls. "A lot of the people I grew up with went there. It would have been like high school all over again." He had no way of foreseeing the irony that one day he would work in a company renowned for its eggheads—in contemporary parlance, nerds. That company was Microsoft.

Against the backdrop of the sixties' counterculture, with hippies proclaiming peace and love and protesters denouncing the Vietnam War, Neil pursued his education. When a friend suggested he take some computer classes, Neil agreed to give it a try. He learned the basics of computer programming and in the summer worked for the Navy Department. Neil shakes his head as he recalls that experience. "We were on-line to a computer running BASIC, so I could type in the commands rather than deal with punch cards. Things were going well, but my hair was a little bit long, and one day the commander called me into his office and told me to cut my hair." In the late sixties, the length of a man's hair was considered an indicator of his political beliefs. For Neil, that job represented a paycheck and the ability to continue his college education. "I cut my hair."

At Northwestern, Neil continued to take computer classes. He learned more about programming languages such as ALGOL and BASIC. As his expertise grew, so did job offers involving computers. At the time, most businesses and colleges used mainframe computers.

When he graduated, Neil had some decisions to make. He says, "There was a lot going on in the country. The draft was on, and I was in the lottery, but my number never came up. I was lucky." His academic ambitions were as strong as ever, so he decided to apply to graduate schools and continue his studies in math and computer science. But first, Neil decided to take a break from intellectual pursuits. He and a few friends took a motorcycle tour of western America and Alaska. Neil remembers it well. "We ended up in Boulder, Colorado. My friends and I moved back into the woods into an old cabin. We sold our motorcycles and bought a four-wheel drive truck." Ever since his teenage years as an Eagle Scout, he had been intrigued by wilderness living.

During his stay in Boulder, a friend of Neil's who was on his way to Alaska visited him. "I'd always wanted to go to Alaska," Neil explains. "I'd read a lot of books about Arctic explorers and I had this incredible feeling that I had been an Arctic explorer in a previous life—it held a powerful attraction for me." One day, Neil just decided to go. He stopped in Seattle, bought some clothing, and boarded a ferry heading for Alaska. As Neil recounts his stay there, his face brightens. "I lived there for a couple of years in a cabin that was in the interior, north of Fairbanks. No electricity, no running water." Neil and another fellow had found an old mining cabin that dated back to 1906, the height of the gold rush years. Neil says proudly, "We fixed it up. We put on a new roof, put in some insulation, and put in a stove just in time for winter."

Neil's cabin was about a mile from the road. Within a five-mile radius there were only about 20 cabins. Neil reminisces about the good times he had there. "We'd all get together either in our cabins, or once a month we'd go into town to socialize. In the summer, we worked in town to make money for the rest of the year. There was a place called the Howling Bog Saloon and everybody would get together and dance and play fiddle music. It was a community and really fun."

One spring, Neil and his cabin mate, who was also his best friend, visited family and friends in Illinois. His friend wanted him to try a kind of meditation he'd just heard about. Soon, they were both taking instruction. Neil says, "It changed our lives. When we were in Alaska we'd write letters to our friends and encourage them to visit Alaska and find the peace that we had. But we knew it wasn't a practical solution because most people don't want to be that isolated." Although Neil declines to say what type of mediation they studied, he felt that, through this practice, he could live anywhere and still have the sense of peace he'd felt in Alaska. Neil was also saddened by the encroachment of oil pipelines on that wilderness. He decided it was time to get back into society and make some contributions. "The whole time I was living in Alaska it was a very physical thing—to stay alive, to cook your own food, and to cut your own wood. We would read books at night, but I wasn't really using my intellect or other abilities. I knew I had been given an intellect and that I was a natural leader."

Neil moved back to Illinois and, for a brief time, worked

as a computer programmer. But, having a career as a programmer didn't really appeal to him. He explains, "It's kind of like living in Alaska. It's living like a hermit. You live your life in a little cubicle; it's isolating." Consequently, Neil went back to Northwestern and got his MBA in finance and accounting. His talent for teaching led him to mentor other students in the computer center. He explains, "All of the class projects consisted of teams of four or five people. I was the only one who knew how to work the computers. We did mathematical modeling and financial plans on the computers—this was before Visi-Calc and personal computers. Because of this, we had a big advantage." Neil's computer skills and leadership abilities were honed by this experience, and looking back, he realizes how much those projects helped prepare him for his career at Microsoft.

When Neil received his MBA from Northwestern, he had many job offers to consider in the areas of management of software and technical resources. Because he wanted to live out West again, he took a position as assistant information systems manager with Digital Equipment Corporation in Colorado Springs, Colorado, where its largest manufacturing plant was located. It was 1979. The PC revolution was brewing, just waiting to take the world by storm. Neil's experience was exhilarating. "I really loved it there. It was a wonderful place to live."

Neil recalls his four years at DEC. "I was about thirty years old and having a great time. I really got into running. I got married while I was there. Everything was going well for about three or four years." But in 1983, things changed. "Digital was a second-generation minicomputer company. In the early 1980s, they started having problems. They did not recognize the future of personal computers." As a result, DEC initiated a hiring and wage freeze. Neil says quietly, "That was the beginning of a downward spiral for the company." Although Neil was still employed, he had a tough decision to make.

A friend who worked at Microsoft encouraged Neil to look into the company. At the time, Microsoft had less than 200 employees. Neil laughs as he remembers their conversation. "He told me Microsoft was located in Bellevue, Washington. I said, 'Where is Bellevue, Washington? I've never even heard of it!' " But Neil's friend was persistent. A Microsoft recruiter called Neil and FedExed him some information and a ticket to fly to Bellevue. Neil says, "I thought it would be a good chance to visit my friend. I stayed in a little hotel next to Microsoft. I remember just sitting there. It was March 1983. Outside, everything was so green and there were flowers everywhere. I went for a drive along Lake Washington in Kirkland. I thought, 'Wow! This is beautiful!' "

Neil faced his first round of interviews. Microsoft has always been very careful about hiring people, and prospective employees often were subjected to five or more interviews. The first person to interview Neil was Steve Ballmer, second in command at Microsoft. Shaking his head, Neil recounts his first interview. "I remember Dave Neir, who was to become financial controller, and I both arrived in the Microsoft lobby the same day. We were both sitting there and I really didn't know much about Microsoft. It didn't have any name recognition at all for me. I was just sitting there waiting for Steve Ballmer to come down. Later, I learned that it's very hard to predict *when* and *where* Steve might show up. Craig Watjen, the treasurer, came down to pick up Dave Neir for his interview. I waited in the lobby for an hour while they were trying to track down Steve." With fondness, Neil says, "That's sort of my perennial story about Steve while I worked with him. 'Where is Steve? We gotta find him! He has a meeting!' "

Eventually, they found Steve. Neil's interview with Steve for the position of database manager went very well. Neil says, "Steve was trying to find out about my ability to be passionate, to be dedicated, and to become really good at something. He wanted to see my overall energy and enthusiasm." During the interview, Steve made it clear that Microsoft was divided into two parts. One part of the company did the software development. Neil says, "I didn't want to be a software developer. I was only 'medium' into software. These people were hard core into it. I had worked at a computer center and at midnight you had to kick the developers out because they would stay all night if you let them—even if you didn't pay them to do it." The other part of Microsoft was its business side, and that's where Neil fit in. They needed people to run it. At the time, Neil had no idea how difficult this would be.

Microsoft made Neil an offer and, as part of the deal, proposed to give him some pieces of paper called "stock options." Neil had no inkling of how these stock options would change his life and the lives of thousands of Microsoft employees. Neil leans forward and says almost confidentially, "I had no idea that they had any value, because in 1983 Microsoft was a private company. They wouldn't show you their financial records. So when some-one says, 'I'm going to give you options for 5,000 shares,' well, you have no idea if it's worth anything if they won't tell you the value of the company."

Neil thought long and hard about the offer. For him, it was a new challenge, in a new industry, in a different part of the country. "I had a great experience at DEC. I was glad I was there. But, I also saw that the minicomputer industry had peaked. DEC had peaked and was on its way down. Data General and Wang and other companies had peaked for the same reason. The PC industry was emerging. I saw that that was where the growth would be and that was where all of the smart people were going. It was really growing quickly and I thought it was a great opportunity."

Life at Microsoft

In April 1983, Neil accepted Microsoft's offer. He was given an office in their building on Northup Way in Bellevue. Neil remembers it well. "They were nice offices. They were paying their bills and it didn't look like they were going out of business any time soon." His concerns were legitimate. In the early days of the personal computer industry, many high-tech companies were started and many of them failed. The competition was fierce, not only to survive but also to emerge as number one. "I was leaving a company that had 100,000 employees and $100 million in revenue for a company that had around $20 million in revenue and 200 employees. But I just had this feeling that it would be a good opportunity for me to get in on the ground floor."

At DEC, employees were given a badge with a number on it. That number allowed everyone to see when that person had joined the company. Neil's number was 71,000. When Neil left, DEC had about 110,000 employees. Neil says, "You kept your number the entire time you were there. I met a guy who was employee number twenty. I used to ask him what it was like when DEC had only twenty employees. There was a reverence in the company for people who had been there for so long. Ken Olsen, founder and CEO of DEC, used to clean the bathrooms back then! He was their Bill Gates; he was their founder. Then it occurred to me that Microsoft was like DEC used to be. It was at the beginning of being a major company. I thought that was pretty cool."

Neil recalls his first few months at Microsoft with a look of disbelief. "We were a private company then. It used to take us about a month to close the books. They'd give a flash report the day after the close of the month. They'd say, 'Flash! This is what we think is going to happen.' The company had two businesses, the OEM [original equipment manufacturers] royalty licensing business and the packaged product business. We had to design two sets of accounting systems." At the time, however, Microsoft had no management information system (MIS). Neil laughs as he recalls the early years at Microsoft. "They were running the company finances on a Tandy personal computer—the TRS-80. Microsoft was about a $20 to $30 million company and they were running on this tiny little computer." Microsoft licensed its products to customers, and it needed a better way to keep track of billing and royalty payments. At the same time, the company was growing rapidly and had many competing priorities, including OEM. "They didn't have any way of doing any of the OEM revenue royalties." Neil explains his amazement, "They were doing a time-share for the packaged products—the manufacturing and the shipping. They had no system for the OEM records."

Shortly after Neil came on board, Microsoft snipped a quote out of the *Wall Street Journal*, blew it up and hung it on the wall. It said, "Microsoft's MS-DOS is becoming the 'de facto standard' for operating systems for the IBM PC." At the time, there were only a few operating systems that buyers could purchase for their personal computers: CP/M 86, UNIX, and one or two others. Neil says, "At this point, about mid-1983, the industry had not yet realized that MS-DOS would become the industry standard. It wasn't even the standard operating system when I joined Microsoft. That was a very significant event when it became the operating system for the IBM PC. We only had a few products—BASIC and other computer language versions. We didn't really have any applications. We were more of an operating system and computer-language company then."

When Neil first spoke to Bill Gates, they discussed ways in which they could manage and evaluate the company's information. Bill understood that a company of that size couldn't run on the PCs available at the time. Neil agreed, and they made the project a top priority. Bill told him to find a platform to manage the corporate information management systems on XENIX, which was an easier and more powerful Microsoft-enhanced version of AT&T's UNIX.

Neil looked at what was available. He needed two solutions, one for each Microsoft operation: the packaged product side of Microsoft, which was high volume and low unit price, and the OEM licenses, which generated royalties. "In a lot of ways, Microsoft was always pushing the limits of building systems for businesses that they were creating. That was an incredible challenge," says Neil. He needed a budget of about $100,000 for hardware and software. Neil called everyone together. He called in Scott Oki from sales, Craig Watjen from finance, and people from other areas of Microsoft. They asked Neil why they were there. He explained that he wanted to tell them his plan and get it approved. They listened politely and told him it sounded good. Neil says, "Afterwards, Steve Ballmer was really upset. He told me, 'Listen! We hired *you* because we thought *you* knew what we needed and you should go out there and do it! You don't *need* to convince *everybody* else. You're supposed to know what to do. Go do it!' "

Neil was stunned. "It was just completely different from anything I'd ever experienced," he says. "No bureaucracy. Total trust. I didn't need permission. At DEC, you had to get consensus for your plans. I just took everything I'd learned at DEC and thought it would work at Microsoft. That turned out to be completely wrong. Microsoft was nothing like that. In fact, it was the total opposite. It took me about a year to figure that out."

Now Neil could implement his plan swiftly and efficiently. He looked at available business systems applications and database systems and picked an application for Microsoft's retail business in packaged products. But Neil thought Microsoft should develop its own system for the OEM business. Neil contracted someone to design and implement the database. It took about six to eight months to finish it. The implementation was so successful that Microsoft hired its designer, Jim Peterson, and he became a well-respected player within the OEM group.

Neil notes, "OEM is still the most profitable business at Microsoft. It was a unique business; no one had ever done it before—licensing software. There were no systems. There were no standards. The contracts were made up as they went along. The information systems had to record the contracts, the ordering schedules, and the quarterly payments. You couldn't just go out and buy a system that could do those kinds of things."

The PC industry continued to grow at breakneck speed. Microsoft was still growing faster than the capabilities of its computers. "We were always behind the curve in trying to run the company on the same PC technology that we were selling to customers. It took almost ten years until the capabilities of the computers finally caught up with the needs of Microsoft. In the early 1990s, we could finally become the showcase company that ran on the same technology we were selling." Today, those products are household names: Word, Excel, Office, and Exchange.

Despite Neil's accomplishments, the next year or so at work was hard for him, and he wondered just where he fit in. The vortex of success that was sweeping up the company made for some unusual problems. He had purchased a condominium close to Microsoft, and his commitment was apparent. He recalls, "Microsoft kept growing. When we were in the Northup building, all of the groups were spread around. The finance group, which I was a part of, was on one floor. But there was no room for me there. So they stuck me in a room with a programmer in the programmer's wing. A lot of people at the time thought Microsoft was a programmer's company. If you weren't a programmer, then you were nobody. The guy I shared the office with wasn't very happy about it. He'd get all upset and go to Steve and yell, "This guy's disturbing us! His phone is ringing and there is nobody here to answer it!" Neil laughs at the memory. "Eventually, they found me another office." A year later, in 1984, Microsoft moved into larger offices across the street, which management thought would accommodate them for five years. Neil says in amazement. "Those offices didn't even accommodate us for one year! That's how rapidly Microsoft continued to grow."

Neil thought Steve Ballmer could help him sort out his job description. But Steve was a very busy man. "Meeting with Steve and trying to understand what I was supposed to do was a big challenge. Most of the time, he didn't show up at meetings. I'd say, 'We're going to go over and buy some software. Here's my plan.' I spent a week preparing the plan so I could get permission to spend money." Neil hunkers over the table and riffles through some pages as he imitates Steve's working style. "Steve would say, 'What are we going to talk about?' and I'd tell him. Then he'd rapidly flip through the pages for only a few seconds. He'd say, 'What else have you got?' " Neil laughs hard remembering his first encounters with Steve. "It was very hard to get Steve's attention." Neil can laugh about it now, but, at the time, he recalls being extremely frustrated.

Designing the data center for Microsoft's computers was a daunting task. Neil remembers Microsoft's early computer room. "When I got to Microsoft, the computer center was what I'll call 'spaghetti.' There were cables everywhere—coming through the ceiling, through the floor—a total mess. Those computers were in a room without air-conditioning! The big computers were kicking off heat, and we called them 'the Microsoft hair dryers.' "

Gordon Letwin, the head programmer in charge of operating systems, did not appreciate Neil stepping into his territory. As Neil began to make much-needed changes, he recalls, "Gordon was the most techie person. The computer center kind of matched his lifestyle, which was chaotic. I had to go in and make peace with him. Everything I wanted to do, Gordon would run to Steve and say, 'No! No! No! We're not doing that!' I would have to fight for everything." Neil looks a bit weary and frustrated as he recalls the turf wars and the fact that he was required to be an expert in both software and hardware.

It was another example of how different Microsoft was from Neil's former employer, DEC, where consensus was the name of the game. Neil says, "To build a data center, all the interested people would be consulted. They'd listen to the needs, design the center, get the contractors, and build it." At DEC, Neil was not called upon to work with hardware. It was a company that had specialists for every job. Neil raps the table. "All of a sudden, at Microsoft, I'm the data center guy, the hardware guy, the software guy, and the business interface guy! I didn't know how to do *all* of those things. I had to figure it out!" It was sink-or-swim time, Microsoft style, except no one seemed to understand that Neil might need a little bit of time to catch his breath or, at the very least, benefit from having a "corporate lifeguard." But Neil was not alone. Due to rapid growth, the many execs and programmers were racing forward alone on "Microsoft time."

Neil's "lifeguard" turned out to be Craig Watjen. He taught Neil how to stay afloat in Microsoft's changing currents. Neil needed to trust his own decisions and act on them—quickly. He did not need consensus. The upside of this turbulent company culture was the trust. Neil says, "It was all very entrepreneurial—very creative and trusting. They would trust you to spend $100,000. If it worked, the next time they'd trust you to spend $200,000. If it hadn't worked, they'd ask you to tell them why it was going to work next time."

While Neil was learning how things worked at Microsoft, he was putting in very long hours. At DEC, he was used to working from 7 A.M. until 5 P.M. Those hours didn't work at Microsoft. Most people came in at 9 A.M., worked all day, and began meetings at 6 or 7 P.M. So Neil began putting in 12-hour days. He also often had to meet with Steve Ballmer on a Saturday or Sunday morning, which was when Steve was available. Neil says, "I was working sixty- to sixty-five-hour weeks. There was a real sense that this was our company. I was an owner of the company, and nobody works harder than the owner. You really want to. At larger companies you have backups if you go on vacation. At Microsoft, there were no backups. The success of the company depended on you being there and making sure it all worked. I liked that. I liked jumping in."

Although Neil liked the heady, adrenaline-rush, creative environment at Microsoft, the long hours began to take a toll on him. He was used to jogging during his lunch hours at DEC. "It kept me healthy, kept me young, and kept the stress down. I started out that way at Microsoft, and then I started working through lunch and having business lunches. After about eight months, I was really stressed out." Neil went to Steve and told him how exhausted he was by the long hours. Neil says simply, "I went through a kind of crisis after I had been there for about a year."

One other area of frustration and stress for Neil was the Microsoft review system. The manager writes up a review of the employee at the same time the employee writes up a review of his or her own performance. A review of 3.0 meant you met the expectations of your position; 4.0 meant you exceeded the expectations; and a review of 5.0, which was rare, meant you far exceeded the expectations. The manager and employee would meet to discuss the reviews.

"Steve has very high expectations," says Neil. "I put down a couple of 4.0s. I had built the computer room, so I put down 4.0. Steve said, '3.0!' I said, 'What do you mean?!' Steve said, 'We expected you to do that!' and then he banged on the table. Everything I'd say, he'd say, 'I expected you to do that!' " Neil laughs and says, "It was really frustrating."

At the end of his first year, Neil was ready to call it quits. He considered going back to DEC, and they would have been more than happy to have him back. Once again, Neil went to Steve. Neil re-creates in an animated voice their meeting: "Steve started banging on the desk and says, 'You're not leaving! We bought the system you recommended and we bought the software. *You* are going to stay here and make it work!' " Neil stops to laugh. "Steve and I had this huge blowup. We were standing in the hall by Bill's office and Bill was out of town. Steve and I were yelling at each other out in the hall and Bill's assistant came out and said, 'You guys have got to get out of the hall. You're too noisy!' So we went into Bill's office and she said we were still too noisy. So we went to the computer room with all of the air-conditioning noise and we were just yelling and screaming at each other. Finally, Steve convinced me that they'd made all of these investments based on *me* and that *I* needed to stay at Microsoft and make sure they worked. He said, 'If you need to do things like running at lunchtime, go do them. Don't kill yourself for the company!' When Bill came back, they gave me a pitch and some more stock options." For all the rough-and-tumble interaction and Neil's many frustrations, this episode made him feel valued, even indispensable.

From that point on, everything got easier for Neil. "I felt accepted as part of the team. I felt a lot of ownership in the company and wanted to stay and make things work. It was okay for me to work out and do what I needed to do. They weren't going to think I wasn't working hard enough or not dedicated enough. After Steve and I argued, our relationship improved. He started appreciating what I was doing. Prior to that, he was telling me I was just doing an average job and I thought I was killing myself! Steve rarely said, 'Great job.' But once you're part of the team, they'll stand behind you and they'll help you. They will allow you to make mistakes and learn from them. The way they rewarded you was to give you more stocks and a good position. But, even then, they still think they can improve things and do better."

Microsoft had made a shrewd decision when they hired Neil. From 1983 to 1994, Neil's abilities, ideas, and achievements helped to propel Microsoft into a global technology company to be reckoned with. As Neil recounts his key contributions to the company, his face flushes with pride and enthusiasm. "I think the most important thing I did was build the information technology that helped the company succeed. But I think my biggest achievement was building the Microsoft Internal Network." Once Microsoft began spinning off subsidiaries, they needed to be connected to headquarters now located in Redmond, Washington, near Bellevue. Scott Oki set up international subsidiaries and Dave Neir put the financial systems in place. Neil and his staff of hundreds implemented the e-mail and computer systems, which enabled everyone—the staff and all the country managers—to be on the Microsoft Network via e-mail and attached documents. Neil points out that the Network was the key to the company's success. "It was the digital nervous system of the company and the thing that made Microsoft *really* work in fifty countries and across twenty-four time zones for thousands of employees. The Network was so good we called it a utility. People just took it for granted."

The Network was done in three phases. First, the Network on the Microsoft campus was designed and checked and rechecked to make sure it worked well. It was finished in six months. Then, all of the U.S. Microsoft Networks were connected to Redmond, Washington, where Microsoft headquarters was then located. After that, the international subsidiaries were connected. Neil says, "We used to have a saying: 'Until you're on the Network, you don't really exist—you're not part of the Microsoft culture and organization.' We looked at the Network as crucial."

Microsoft was the first company to use transatlantic fiber-optic cables. They had a fiber-optic cable run from AT&T in New Jersey to Seattle and then from Seattle to England and Ireland. From there, it went to the European continent. All the data and e-mail would flow through those systems. Products were first developed in English and later translated into other languages.

Neil traveled to other countries to better understand which Microsoft businesses would work best there. He managed a team that installed the networks. "We had to figure out what the offices were going to do, how much bandwidth and how much support they would need," says Neil. The Second and Third World countries presented an extreme challenge for Neil and his staff of hundreds. The developing countries' Network infrastructure was not very good. They did not have powerful or reliable phone lines, and security was a problem. In many of these countries, government permission was required in order to use high-tech equipment. "We used to have a guy we called our Network Rambo. He would go into South American countries, Eastern Europe, and Korea and smuggle in modems and tools to get the Network up and running," says Neil.

Neil points out that they used the cookie-cutter approach. In other words, they used the same Microsoft Network operating systems, infrastructure, architecture, protocols, and applications for every subsidiary in the world. Neil says, "We made it very easy to support—we knew exactly what was there and we knew how to fix it. The cookie-cutter approach helped us build very quickly because we didn't have to reinvent it for each country."

The Network was and is critical to Microsoft's amazing success, and Neil takes justifiable pride in his accomplishments. I asked him to try to define in retrospect what he believes were key reasons for Microsoft's phenomenal success. He thinks for a moment and says, "If there were nine good things about a product and one bad thing, Bill and Steve would focus on the one bad thing we needed to improve. At some places, they'll focus on the nine good things and worry about the one bad thing later. Microsoft wasn't like that; they wanted to fix it and make an even better product."

At Microsoft, people were not expected to take things personally—it was business. "You could have strong opinions, you could attack and defend things because it's not about you—it's about ideas, business proposals, and business issues. You are expected to remain friends after a business confrontation. This results in good business decisions. At most companies, if someone worked a long time on a project, they would fund it and keep it going in some form. There is an unwritten rule at most companies that you don't get critical and confrontational—you try to work around people's egos and weaknesses and fragileness."

Neil learned invaluable business lessons from Steve and Bill. He says, "They taught me that if you're going to be world class at something, you've got to focus on just a few things. We would figure out how to make those things work and make the system successful. We had to make sure that the Network and all of the resources needed to develop software were working well and didn't inhibit anyone." Neil and Microsoft wanted to be certain the business systems were tracking the sales and the OEM contracts. At the same time, they also needed to ensure that they were getting paid and meeting customer expectations. The customers and the technical support system were equally important to them.

Another thing Neil learned from Bill and Steve is what he calls relentlessness, or persistence. "They taught me that you should never give up. If you have a goal, work hard at it from many angles, and if it's important to the success of the company, then keep going. They also taught me that you need to run a business very critically and objectively. There has to be honesty, and people have to be able to speak frankly about problems without people getting defensive or taking things personally. That's very hard to do. It took me about a year and a half to get used to having my ideas torn apart and looked at critically. They're your plans, your ideas."

From Bill and Steve, Neil also learned how to set daily priorities. Every day at Microsoft he would have hundreds of things coming his way, and he had to figure out which four or five of those things were most important. Neil says emphatically, *"Every day* you've got to make those decisions; otherwise, you could be very, very busy, but really not working at the right sets of things."

After more than 10 years with Microsoft, Neil decided to retire. He was very wealthy and could afford to do whatever he wanted. But why did he leave when he was at the height of his success? With complete honesty, Neil says, "The stress on my marriage made me realize that working at Microsoft had really affected my personal life. I really needed to depressurize from Microsoft." Neil has an apt analogy that describes how and why he changed as a result of his Microsoft experience. "This is the way I like to think about it: If you took a dog to somebody's house to live, when he grew up, he'd be a house dog. If you took that dog to the wilderness of Alaska, he'd turn into a wolf because that's what he'd have to do to survive. So Microsoft creates wolves in the sense that they teach you to survive. They create people who can work hard, can be really strong, can get things done, and can take adversity. They can fight for their ideas and make things happen and succeed—against all odds. It changes you because you become a lot more—well, expedient. I can't really think of the right descriptor. The downside of that is that it carries over into your personal life. But you don't want to be a boss and ruthless in your personal life. You want to be completely different. My marriage ended, in a large part, because the way I was at Microsoft dominated a large part of my life."

In addition to this, Neil saw, firsthand, how brief and fleeting life can be. "My boss at Microsoft, Frank Gaudette, was the chief financial officer. He got cancer and died within about six months. I would go visit him in the hospital and he'd say to me, 'Nothing's guaranteed.

You really need to live your life now.' He had lived his whole life working hard and saving his money. He was going to retire within a year. He'd built a big house on Lake Washington and he never got to move into it. He'd saved up all of his fun time for the future and he never got to use it."

Neil also realized that with his financial independence, he could go back to what he loved doing best: teaching. He says with fondness for the world of learning, "I love education, I love working with young people, and I love the cycle of education—summers are free, and every twelve weeks there is a break between quarters. I like evangelizing about how important the information technology is in the new economy. We have what I call 'beige-collar workers' because they work with beige-colored equipment and they are going to be our next middle class. The blue-collar class is going downhill fast. It's a new era."

Neil has a message for young people. "We're really just at the beginning of the Information Age. Get as much education as you can. Education, more than any other issue, is going to define your quality of life and income levels. But make sure that your education is practical. Make sure that you have computer literacy and that you know how to use information technology tools. The jobs are going to need people who know how to research, evaluate, and publish information in all its aspects. Twenty years ago, the best people went into law. Fifteen years ago, they went into medicine. Over the last ten to fifteen years, they've gone into electronics. After software came the Internet. It was exciting for me to start in the software industry twenty years ago and watch and help it grow. It was not only exciting, it allowed me to work with very bright people."

I asked Neil, "Would you do your Microsoft experience all over again?" He breaks into a grin and says, "Of course!" as if it were the most obvious answer in the world. His look says, "Why would anyone think otherwise?" Indeed, Microsoft wasn't perfect, but for Neil, it was the right place at the right time to make use of his considerable talents.

Life after Microsoft

Today, many years after his early dream of becoming a professor, Neil is back in the educational world. He is the dean of Technology Services at Bellevue Community College in Washington. Neil helped get funding from the National Science Foundation so the college could create the Center for Information Technology in Advanced Education. The goal is to establish a two-year degree for electronic technicians to enable them to acquire the skills to maintain, operate, and repair the tools of the new technology. Neil says, "We cannot create these skilled workers fast enough." Neil loves to evangelize about the importance of technology in education.

In addition, Neil gives talks at educational technology conferences, which provide information and speakers on the role of technology in education. One of his topics is called "The Information Revolution," in which Neil describes the previous revolutions that led to this monumental transformation of our time. He reviews the development of the written word some 4,000 years ago and the invention of movable type in the fifteenth century, which gave millions of people access to the written word. Then he moves forward to our time, discussing the revolution fostered by the PC and the Internet. Neil creates a context to help people understand the current information revolution and how crucial it is for education. Neil serves on the IT Advisory Board, which oversees virtual universities on the Internet in 13 western states.

Neil still indulges the right side of his brain. When he isn't out riding his Harley, he makes films, a skill he learned from the film school at the University of Washington. His documentary film, *Biker Dreams,* is about the Harley subculture. It follows a Seattle couple who rode to a biker rally in Sturgis, South Dakota. The film relates how the trip, and the people they met along the way, changed one couple's relationship. *Biker Dreams* premiered at the Santa Barbara Film Festival and has been shown at other major film festivals.

DAVE NEIR

"The CPA"

Microsoft: 1983–1993

International Financial Controller

Director, Intercontinental Operations

Senior Director, Business Operations,
Microsoft Press

DAVE NEIR

"The CPA"

Dave Neir is a CPA, and he is analytical and sharp. He has given up the three-piece suit of his profession and dresses casually in retirement. He is only in his early 40s. As a devout Christian, Dave respects the Golden Rule in both business and personal endeavors. Although neighborly and obliging, he is a private person who avoids the spotlight.

Dave was hired by Microsoft in 1983. Because he wanted to work someplace close to home, Dave found Microsoft in the Yellow Pages and through the Bellevue Chamber of Commerce. He had never heard of the company before.

As financial controller and later as director of Intercontinental Operations, Dave brought a business structure to the newly formed International Division. Bob O'Rear referred to him as a "godsend" for Microsoft's international business.

Dave retired in 1993, and today he enjoys spending time with his three children and helping his wife pursue her interests. He now has time to contribute his skills to the operation of his local Church of Christ and to engage in outdoor activities at his restored wilderness resort.

The Path to Microsoft

Dave Neir grew up in Kirkland, Washington, and attended public schools. He was just an average math student. In the summers he worked at a grocery store for a manager who would tell him, "If you're not sweatin', you're not workin'." Dave says, "It was good training. I never resented it. Everyone worked hard. He was a good manager." After high school, Dave attended Western Washington University, where he studied psychology. A professor noticed his aptitude for the subject and gave him access to the resources of the entire psychology department. At the same time, Dave took an accounting class. Dave laughs and says, "It was boring—basic bookkeeping. I either dropped out or flunked out—I can't remember. That was the beginning of my 'stellar' accounting career."

In 1976, Dave married and attended the University of Washington. While there, he had a practical turn of mind and changed his major to accounting. "I wanted to start a family and I didn't think psychology would pay the bills, in the long run." So Dave signed up for his first financial accounting class and, despite his previous encounters with bookkeeping, really enjoyed it, especially the legal aspects of the subjects. In 1977, he received his degree in accounting from Seattle University. During that time he also worked full time at an accounting firm and at night studied for the CPA exam.

Dave spent three years in public accounting at two firms in the Seattle area. He says, "It was a nice springboard into business. I had a chance to meet clients and customers from different industries."

From 1980 to 1983, Dave worked as the financial controller for Standard Aero Ltd., a company based in
Canada, which manufactured and distributed worldwide
a variety of aviation components ranging from oil filters,
bombs, and military supplies to whole planes and heli-
copters. Dave says, "I got a lot of international experience
doing that." In 1983, Dave helped the company consolidate its U.S. and Canadian headquarters and move to
Minneapolis in order to centralize North American operations. "I spent eight months moving the offices back
there. But I didn't want to move. Neither did Suzanne."

Dave decided that he'd like to work for a high-tech company that was close to where he lived. He did not want to
commute. "There were a lot of prospects around, but I
saw high tech as a budding industry with many more
opportunities. I was not a technology person, but I
enjoyed playing on minicomputers." He found a company
called Microsoft in the Yellow Pages and checked it out
through the Bellevue Chamber of Commerce. He remembers it well. Microsoft fit his criteria. "They were close to
my home and they were a high-tech company. They were
a small company with about 200 employees. I'd never
heard of them, but since I lived nearby, I went to visit
them on Northup Way and I found they were looking for
someone with international experience."

Dave went for a series of interviews at Microsoft, six in
all. He interviewed with Steve Ballmer five times. "For six
days in a row I'd go back to see them. I'd visit more people, get the grand tour, and they'd say, 'Come back
tomorrow.' And I would. By the sixth day I didn't know
what they were thinking. Finally, Steve sat down and
said, 'Have we convinced you to join the company?' I
looked at him and said, 'Steve, I was ready to join the first
day. I liked what I saw—great people and a great opportunity.' Steve said, 'Oh, we thought you were going to be

a hard sell. You wasted five days of our time! But, you'll join us?' " Dave joined Microsoft in April 1983 as International's financial controller.

Life at Microsoft

Microsoft gave Dave two offices, one in Finance and one in International, the division that had just been formed by Scott Oki. They also gave Dave something called stock options. Dave laughs and recalls his reaction. "It was nice, but I had no idea what this company could really do back then. So I thought the options were actually *worthless.* But Scott Oki always told me, 'If you have a choice between salary and options, always take the stock options. This is going to be a really great company when it grows up.' He had a lot of foresight. He'd been at Hewlett-Packard and had the background to see the potential of the options."

His first day on the job, someone gave Dave a calculator to use. Dave says, "It was really weird, though, because I could never get it to give me the right answers. I finally returned it only to learn that it was a calculator used by programmers! It worked with base-eight numbers." In his first months, Dave used an original IBM PC with a floppy drive. "A really exciting day for me was when I received a new top-of-the-line one with five megabytes of hard drive."

Employees at Microsoft dressed very casually, in shorts and T-shirts. Dave smiles and says. "For five years I wore a three-piece suit and tie to work. I was from an accounting background. It just really felt out of character for a CPA to wear jeans and a T-shirt to work. I looked out of place for years."

Ironically, given Dave's desire not to commute, he was

soon spending 70 percent of his time traveling. As International's controller, Dave was expected to bring a business structure to this newly formed International division. He says, "International's marketing staff of Scott Oki, Bob O'Rear, Beth Danners, and others was excellent, but they lacked the infrastructure needed to run an international company: export licensing, shipping, inventory control, invoicing, financial systems, and so on." At the time, Microsoft's domestic accounting was done on a Radio Shack PC using 8-inch floppy disks. "While it was leaps and bounds better than the manual system prevalent then, we can all laugh at it now," Dave notes. International systems were a little tougher to assemble because of all the different currencies. Microsoft used ALTOS microcomputers and REAL WORLD software, which had been developed in the United States. "Although it was not designed for international application, the group was able to make it work," Dave says. "All the subsidiaries used the identical software and hardware, which made it easier for us to support. Many times I'd get calls at 2 A.M. or while on the road from someone really needing support. The identical systems allowed us to close all the financial accounts three days after the end of each month and electronically transfer and consolidate information. That was pretty nifty stuff back then!"

After Scott and Bob became comfortable with Dave, he thought their time was best spent on sales and marketing. Dave handled the rest. Microsoft had settled on having one huge warehouse in Germany that would feed everything in Europe. Jim Towne, then president, and Steve Ballmer had approved the plan. Dave says, "It didn't make any sense to me. We had to do it differently. We had to have warehouses in other countries to provide local products and good customer service." At the time, doing business in Europe meant dealing with different currencies, banks, languages, laws, and customs. "My forte was bringing in a business structure: how you actually set up offices, how you employ people, and all of that. No one knew that in England leases are for twenty-four years, different from other countries." Microsoft's major competitor at the time, Lotus, used the huge central warehouse model. "But it drove customers crazy," Dave says. "It took them forever to get products out of the central warehouse to customers. And customers in Italy wanted to pay in lire, France wanted to pay francs, and they were being invoiced in dollars and pounds."

Dave took his business plan for multiple warehouses to Steve Ballmer, a plan that Scott Oki had wanted all along. "But I had to sell it," says Dave. He remembers his meeting with Steve Ballmer. "It was really my first confrontation with Steve. We talked for an hour in this small, little office. Steve would get up and pace back and forth, yell and scream, and pound his fist—classic Steve. Finally, he sat down and said, 'Yes, you're right. But I'm not going to tell you why you're right.' To this day I have no idea why Steve agreed to the change. But all of the sudden, the basis for structuring an international business changed! It set the tone and it worked. Software can seem like such an intangible thing. Really, it's a license agreement. But the effect of having a warehouse in each country gave the people there a tangible concept of what they were selling, and they really felt committed. They had the inventory in the warehouse—they could touch it and they could see it. They could go to the warehouse and show the products to customers. Or take a box and deliver it."

Dave enjoyed working with Scott and Bob. "We didn't do memos—it was all spoken and efficient. They were both always on top of things and easy to work with. Even at headquarters you were pretty free to do what you needed to do. There was very little bureaucracy. You very rarely had to justify your decisions. Everybody trusted everybody else to do what was right. Things moved very quickly."

In 1984, Dave went to Ireland to negotiate with the Irish government to establish offshore manufacturing of software. Dave had researched other offshore manufacturing in Europe. "At that point Microsoft was not that well known," Dave says. "We met with the Irish Minister of Treasury and he said, 'Well, who is Microsoft? We are discussing millions of dollars of tax grants and I'd like to know who you are before we sign the papers.' I told him to turn on his computer. He did and the screen showed MS-DOS Microsoft. I told him that's who we were. That's how we'd always introduce ourselves to computer users who had never heard of Microsoft."

Although Dave enjoyed working in International, he was well aware of the feelings at Microsoft U.S. about the international division. "U.S. was focused solely on the growing domestic market. To them, International was a thorn in their side and not worthy of spending any extra time on. It wasn't personal. Everything that was done in International was unusual and outside of the domestic routine. While U.S. sold and supported only English-language products, we had to translate, manufacture, and ship all the same products, but in a hundred different languages. The U.S. market and resulting operations were simple compared to the complexities of our international divisions. We had individual P&Ls for each subsidiary. That pushed accountability and responsibility down in the organization—much further than in the U.S. organization. The international group always had a spirit of healthy competition. France and Germany always tried to beat each other in monthly sales, but if one found a better way of doing something, they would immediately pass it on to the other. As a whole, all the subsidiaries worked like that. The U.S. group lacked that competitive and cooperative aspect."

Dave enjoyed setting up the international offices. He says, "A misconception Americans have is that we are superior and have all the answers. American businesses don't realize that there are a lot of smart people offshore. You just have to go to the countries, find these people, and hire them. We were good at attracting and hiring the right kind of people. We'd hire a good general manager and then the whole office would have the right work ethic. The first core people were very important since they would set the pace, expectations, and work ethic."

During his first year at the company, Jim Towne had a talk with Dave and Scott. "He gave us a lecture on ethics. Very interesting. Here we are, in the president's office, and Microsoft is a very small company. He gave us a lecture on ethics in the business world. His message was that we were in International, traveling around the world, and we should never do anything to embarrass the company. He told us to do things right—be moral. For him to have the presence of mind to do that was pretty neat. It showed respect for people. I always remembered that lecture."

Dave really enjoyed his first year at Microsoft. He says, "It was an opportunity to design, implement, and develop an international company from the ground up. There were no barriers or prescribed methods. International and financial systems were nonexistent, as were foreign offices except for the branch we had in London. Within a month I wrote a business plan on how to structure the businesses and international company. Scott Oki and I agreed on philosophies for doing business. Once Bill approved where an office should be located, based on customers or strategic importance, then I'd work with Carl Stork or Bob O'Rear to make it happen. We'd find facilities, organize distribution, hire employees, train them, install systems with Richard Hevron, and handle all the local legal requirements. I coordinated everything that wasn't sales and marketing."

About five months after Dave joined in 1983, Microsoft sales were phenomenal. Dave recalls, "Dave Corning, who handled budgeting, Craig Watjen, the CFO, Neil Evans, director of MIS, and I were sitting in a small conference room trying to plan the future. What was the future going to hold for this company? What will the sales be for Microsoft? Neil wanted to know if I was going to put in MIS systems and what I was looking at for sales and employee head count. Here we are, all these financial gurus mapping it out and indicating that we would be at half a billion dollars in the next seven years. Then we stepped back and looked at it and we laughed and said, 'You got to be kidding! This is nuts. There's no way it's gonna happen! There's no way this company can be half a billion in seven years! Actually, it *surpassed* that."

When Frank Gaudette joined the company in 1983 as head of finance and administration for the whole company, he changed Dave's title to Director of International Finance and Accounting. It was a promotion. Dave says, "It was nice of him to do that, but it didn't change my job, which was to build International into a large company. That's what I did for a number of years." But in 1988, President Jon Shirley asked Dave to work directly for Jeremy Butler, VP responsible for International. Scott Oki had moved to Domestic and Dave had been reporting to Frank. Dave says, "Jeremy's group was closer to sales. They asked me to take over as director of Intercontinental Operations, which Bob O'Rear had handled. The organization was in great shape. The new markets were everything except Europe, the United States, and a few Asian countries. I told them I was not a sales guy. I was concerned that I didn't have the necessary sales and marketing experience. I had a nice meeting with President Jon Shirley, and he tried to convince me to take the job. He said, 'Don't worry about it. I don't want a salesperson. You have salespeople. I want somebody who can *run* it. Bob's group is in top-notch shape in sales and marketing.' He explained to me that I did have the skill set to run it. I took the job and loved it!" Dave handled general management of the subsidiaries in his territory along with long-term strategy and sales to the emerging markets.

Dave spent most of his time traveling. His markets were tough ones: South America, Africa, the Middle East, Canada, Australia, and most parts of Asia. "It was really difficult to get the products translated into some of the languages such as Hebrew and Farsi. But I had a lot of good people working for me. They worked very hard and knew their areas. There were so many different cultures, business practices, laws, and conflicts. You had to be really patient to work through all of that."

The travel was demanding. And Dave didn't see much of his family. He says, "I was traveling like crazy, and I never appreciated it from my kids' point of view. One time I was working in the office—just my normal working hours—I'd go in before the kids woke up and come home after 9 or 10 P.M. I happened to see Cassandra, my daughter, one day. She said, 'Oh, you're here!' She assumed I was traveling and had no idea I was even in the country. I'd been home all week and she didn't even know it. That was a real eye-opener." Another time, Dave had been gone for over a month, and when his family picked him up at the airport, he didn't recognize his children. "Just in that short time they had changed so much," Dave says ruefully.

"If you asked my kids what I did for a living they'd say I worked for Microsoft, but beyond that they really didn't know. For the most part, they were sheltered from that.

So even though I worked at Microsoft, they didn't really learn much about software or computers. But I do think my attitude about work was important. I loved my job at Microsoft and I brought that home. Hopefully, my work ethic and the enjoyment of my work has influenced them," Dave says.

In 1991, Dave was asked to move to Germany to take over responsibility for finance and administration in the central European region. Serious problems were emerging because Microsoft had outgrown the financial and operational structure established in 1983. Germany, for instance, had started with only 5 employees, and by 1991 there were 500. In addition, a few senior management people needed to be replaced and the staff needed a morale boost. The time had come to restructure the business and to remotivate the employees. Microsoft leased a nice house for Dave in Munich and he commuted between Germany and America. "I would be in Germany every week, come back on Saturday morning to watch my kids' soccer games, and on Sunday afternoon I'd hop back on the plane to Germany. I did that for a year, except for summer when the rest of the family spent three months in Germany. The tougher task than replacing senior managers was remotivating the staff. Within a year, we had reduced the employee turnover rate from more than twenty percent to a single digit. This was especially rewarding since it was accomplished with no increase in compensation or benefit levels. I implemented a new regional business structure for International that resulted in centralizing distribution and more efficient billing practices."

By 1992, Dave was tired of traveling. He says, "I wanted to stay home and see my family." He went to work at Microsoft Press. "I became senior director of Business

Operations at Microsoft Press. I could stay on the main campus in Redmond and report to Elton Welke, a wonderful person. He was easy to talk to and reason with. He was very open to different opinions and ideas." Dave took his assignment from Frank Gaudette, who wanted him to build the international business for Press and make it profitable. "I spent a year there going through the distribution structure for U.S. and International and setting up MIS systems and business practices. Press was its own company in many respects—in fact, the largest publishing company this side of the Mississippi. The division created products, manufactured, distributed, and handled sales and marketing. I was responsible for expanding the international publishing division and making it profitable. Because Press was located in Redmond, I could take a big break from traveling."

In 1993, while still at Press, Dave decided to retire. "The day I left Microsoft Press to retire, my last meeting was with Frank. That day we celebrated his remission from cancer. He asked me to reconsider leaving the company, and he told me if I ever did reconsider, I'd have a place there as long as he was around. One of the sadder days of my life came a few months later when Frank passed away from the cancer he had fought so hard to overcome. He was a great boss and a great friend." Dave recalls, "Frank and I used to sit for hours and hours and talk about bureaucracy. We wondered if it was possible to grow a company beyond 3,000 people and not have bureaucracy. What was it that created bureaucracy in a company? We decided that bureaucracy grows because managers don't develop the trust they should have in the decision-making ability of their employees. You have people you don't know, and you start to lose faith in their abilities. That created bureaucracy, and we never did find the secret to avoiding it.

"I left Microsoft because it was getting too big. A staff of 15,000 slows down the wheels of progress. We couldn't avoid bureaucracy. I remember many times holding large meetings with a room full of people, and everybody would agree on a course of action except for one person, and that one person would say no, and then the whole process stopped for *one* person. Maybe the person said no because they didn't understand, or maybe they just had a bad day. It got to the point where it was very frustrating. It was cumbersome. We'd be in meetings all the time. We weren't free to create and develop as we had been in the early years. Scott and I used to go out, grab a burger, talk, and get things done. I'm an implementer. I'll get a plan, work it out, and nothing will stop me from implementing that plan. It will be done and done on time. That's how I worked. Then I started hitting bureaucratic roadblocks. It wasn't fun anymore."

In the 10 years that Dave was at Microsoft, the company grew from 200 people to 15,000 people and $3.3 billion in sales. "In the early years, you could make decisions and get immediate feedback on how well you did or didn't do. I always said that *one* year at Microsoft was like *ten* years at any other company. You could do so much and learn so much in a short period of time."

Dave recalls Bill Gates in the early days. "I remember Bill's beat-up brown Jaguar always sitting in the same parking spot. I don't think they ever had to sweep the ground beneath it! Meetings with Bill were not something I looked forward to. With Bill, you had to know the numbers, be confident in what you were talking about, and be ready to be hammered on. I handled the meetings pretty well. Most were about approving long-term strategic plans and annual budgets. Requesting head count and marketing funds were always controversial topics, and Bill would rule with an iron hand when they came up."

But Bill had a very human side. Dave laughs, "One night I was working late in the London office with Dave Frasier, the GM. In the middle of the night we got a phone call from Bill. He said, 'I'm glad I found someone there. I missed my flight from London to Seattle and I have no money.' I was incredulous. Bill said, 'The security guard gave me some money to dial you. I need a place to stay and some money.' It was classic Bill. He had nothing: no money, no credit cards. He didn't plan to be there! He'd simply missed a connecting flight and was stranded. We always worried about Bill being kidnapped also. He hated the attention associated with bodyguards. His greatest asset in the early years was his appearance. Bill could walk through the airport and no one would even pay attention to a rumpled young man.

"Microsoft has been successful because of the great products, the top-notch people they hire, and the work environment. Underachievers are washed out by peer pressure within eighteen months. The commitment to hard work and long hours was the basic underpinning of Microsoft's success," Dave says. "It would be a 'Velvet Sweatshop' for people who hate it. You do work hard. A lot of people join the company because they have this glorious image of it, but you had to work very hard to last."

Although the world of high tech is ultralogical, pragmatic, and moves at warp speed, Dave never felt any pressure as a devout Christian at Microsoft. "I never felt ridiculed or looked down upon," says Dave. "I always had time for Sunday services and enjoyed the opportunity to meet other Christians around the world."

Dave sums up: "Microsoft wasn't a grind. It was enjoyable. Even though I worked long and unusual hours, I had fun doing it. We all had a personal commitment to make Microsoft successful."

Life after Microsoft

After devoting so much time to his career, Dave enjoys retirement. He drives in car pools, sets up computer labs at his children's school, and organizes the family's day. He is happy to support his wife Suzanne's interests as she supported his career at Microsoft for 10 years. They are very diligent in their efforts not to spoil their children and to teach them about work and managing their money. "These are habits that were formed long before I went to Microsoft," says Dave.

As an active member in the Church of Christ, Dave donates his considerable accounting skills and makes time to help maintain the buildings.

In 1996, Dave and Suzanne began to renovate a 100-year-old resort, which was formerly the Idlewood Resort on Fish Lake in eastern Washington, for their own use. Friends are invited to stay and go fishing, hiking, and engage in other outdoor activities.

For Dave, financial independence gives him time to be with his family. "Before we know it, the kids will be all grown up. Now we both have the time to enjoy them."

IDA COLE

"The Independent"

Microsoft: 1984–1990

Director, International Products

Director, International Marketing

Vice President, Applications

IDA COLE

"The Independent"

Originally from Virginia, Ida Cole has retained her quiet Southern charm and lilting accent. She is warm, enthusiastic, and highly personable. Her keen intellect and decisiveness are readily apparent. An original thinker, she ignores passing ideas and fads.

Ida Cole has worked with two of the most brilliant minds in the world of high tech: Steven Jobs of Apple and Bill Gates of Microsoft. At Apple, Ida was a marketing director in a company that was changing the world of information technology. In 1984, Microsoft hired Ida as its first senior female executive: vice president of Applications, a job she took over from Bill Gates. In 1986, Ida became director of International Products. In both Applications and International, Ida's divisions were enormously successful and profitable.

In 1990, Ida retired and renovated one of Seattle's older and cherished landmarks, the Paramount Theater, which was due to be torn down. Seattle residents and visitors now enjoy touring Broadway performances and concerts of all types at the theater.

The Path to Microsoft

Ida Cole's parents raised her to be independent, a novel approach when she was growing up in the fifties and sixties. Her father, an electrical engineer, thought his daughters were as smart as any boys. Ida recalls, "We started drawing fulcrums on the dining room table when I was eight years old. Although my parents assumed that my sister and I would marry, there was never an assumption that somebody was going to take care of us."

After graduating from high school, Ida left Virginia to go to the University of Massachusetts. She says, "I really wanted to get away from home and be on my own." She practiced what her parents had taught her about independence and education. Later, she received her MBA from Pepperdine University in California.

Young, well educated, and carefree, Ida became an airline stewardess for United Airlines in 1968. She smiles and says, "I did that for a couple of years. It was kind of a lark. If you wanted that kind of life, it wasn't something you could put off, because you had to be hired between the ages of twenty and twenty-six. You had to leave if you got married or turned thirty-two, whichever came first. It was just a job, not a career like it is now."

Ida was living in San Francisco when she married and had to give up her job for United. Her husband was drafted out of graduate school in 1970, and they moved to Fort Ord, California, where her husband did his tour of duty. Jobs were scarce due to a recession. Ida had taken some programming courses in college, but her only computer language was FORTRAN II. With characteristic pluck, Ida says, "There was a job opening for 'junior programmer' so I decided that's what I would be.

"I managed to talk my way into an entry-level job and started learning my skills," Ida says. In 1973, she went to work for Bank of America, where she performed world-wide profitability analysis and worked on time-share computers. In 1977, she landed a job at TymShare in a group called Consulting and Professional Services. That group designed custom systems for people who would then run those systems on TymShare's centralized computers. It was there that Ida learned her management skills. She says, "In five years I went from programmer to project manager to national manager of the technical group."

But Ida realized that the world of computing was changing. "In 1980, I saw an Apple II running VisiCalc and I knew that the time-sharing world was *over*. We were charging $5,000 a month for time-sharing services that could be done in a package that someone could own for $2,500."

By 1980, Apple was a very hot company and Ida wanted in. "Apple was getting about 1,000 unsolicited resumes a week," she remembers. "I didn't know anybody who worked for the company." Serendipity stepped in—one of Ida's neighbors went to work at Apple as a director of engineering. He recruited Ida, and in 1981, Ida was "in."

At Apple, Ida's first job was manager of Applications Development. Six months later she was made director of Applications Software, and she had to juggle both marketing and software development. Apple was experimenting with Special Delivery Software, which was software developed by other people and tested and marketed by Apple. Ida says, "The sales force didn't like it. It didn't look like Apple software. The first thing I did was weed out that software. We really concentrated on our bread-and-butter software for the Apple II and the Apple III." In addition, Ida oversaw product, product design and development, marketing, and distribution.

"I loved the work environment there," Ida says, smiling at the memories. "It was very hard work, but there was also a sense of fun. It was a zany place. There was a sense that we were out to change the world, and we were all very young. We truly *believed*. All companies take their culture from the top, and Steve Jobs was very flamboyant. He is the most charismatic person I have ever known. He's almost Svengali-like. Sometimes I'd leave a meeting with Steve and not really understand what I had agreed to!"

But Apple would not continue to lead the technology revolution. Ida explains, "I think Apple's huge mistake in the market and the reason they have not really flourished is that Apple was always a software company and refused to own up to it. They always thought they were a hardware company—it never was. The hardware was only a cleverly designed delivery vehicle. It was very difficult to be a software person, as I was, in what was perceived as a hardware company."

At Apple, one of Ida's bright stars, Jeff Raikes (who is now a high-level executive at Microsoft), left and headed to Seattle to work for Microsoft. "He and I went through his decision-making process," Ida recalls. I always loved mentoring him—he's so smart and a wonderful person. He was just a baby then. He'd been at Apple a year before me and had come straight from Stanford." Over the next few years, Ida had many dealings with Microsoft and got to know the company well.

In spite of Microsoft's growing success, Ida had no desire to work for the company. She was very happy at Apple. But in 1984, she went through a divorce. At the same time, a project she had led at Apple was canceled. It demanded a faster and better chip than was available then, and a satisfactory one wouldn't come out in time for the project to continue. Ida looked around Apple to decide what she could do next. "About that time," she says, "I began to think that I could look beyond Apple. I'd never really thought of that before."

That fall, Jeff Raikes attended a conference in the San Francisco Bay Area, and he and Ida had dinner together. Ida remembers their conversation about Microsoft: "Jeff said, 'Bill has been looking for a vice president of Applications. Would you come up and interview for it?' I had no interest in going to the Pacific Northwest, but I thought it might be a good idea to test out my interviewing skills. It had been a long time since I'd been interviewed. So, I said to Jeff, 'Oh, why not?!' "

Ida flew to Bellevue, Washington, for her set of interviews at Microsoft. She laughs and with a twinkle in her eye says, "They were serious about it! I wasn't serious. They called me back for another set of interviews. The interviews at Microsoft are just grueling. They went on for days and days!" After some deliberation, Ida began to think seriously about working for Microsoft. "It got me back into software, and that's really where I wanted to be," says Ida. "I was a little disenchanted with Apple, not because I didn't love it there—I did—but because I saw that it was going to be very difficult to continue to succeed at Apple. Our group was becoming obsolete."

Life at Microsoft

Feeling that it was time for a fresh start, Ida accepted the job offer from Microsoft. But she was realistic about the reasons for the offer. "I think Microsoft had other reasons for looking at me. They were looking at a military contract and they had no women VPs—no women in the upper ranks. I think I was probably the best candidate they had seen to date." Government contracts required compliance with affirmative action programs. There needed to be a certain number of women and minorities in ranking positions for Microsoft to win contracts. "But I don't think Bill was quite ready to give up running Applications," Ida recalls. "It was very difficult for me because I was the first person to come in and run Bill's baby, which was Applications."

Right from the start, Ida's working relationship with Bill was strained. Ida says, "Bill had told me that he wanted to be in charge of product specification, but then he'd come to me and say things like, 'You haven't been involved in the product specifications at all!' I think it was harder for him to let go than he had originally thought," says Ida.

"Jon Shirley was the president of Microsoft and I was a vice president, so I assumed I worked for Jon. I didn't realize until far too late that I worked for Bill. I had started working on his products. Early on, he had let me know that I was supposed to run the place and make sure it ran well. But I didn't know how to keep him more involved. It took me a while to figure it out." Ida recalls the frustration she felt. "The idea of what I should be doing had changed, and nobody had really thought it out. My idea was to build a good organization and get the products out." Bill was chairman and CEO and was intensely involved in the product groups.

Although Ida was the only executive female involved in a product, she thinks that was only part of the problem with Bill. "He was so young then," Ida says. "He was only twenty-nine years old. People work best with people they can be comfortable with. He was never really comfortable around me, and I would imagine he still isn't. But there's a lot of respect."

After Ida had been at Microsoft for seven months, she discovered a mass in her abdomen. She'd only been in the Seattle area a short time, so she went to her OB-GYN at Stanford. "It was a very scary time," says Ida. The ultrasound showed a tumor on her ovary that would have to be removed. "I had no pain," Ida says, "but with ovarian cancer there's no pain until the very last stages." It was early September and Ida was scheduled for a road trip to introduce the first version of Excel for Macintosh. "I asked the doctor if it would make any difference to my health and well-being if I waited two weeks to have the surgery. He said that it would be okay. We had told the world that Excel was coming out the end of September. I was not trying to be macho. Everybody else was stressed to the max. I didn't tell my staff or anyone else about my condition. There was no reason to add to their stress levels." Ida did inform Jon and Bill that she was scheduled for surgery. Ida recalls, "I did half of the country for the road show on September 29, and I did the West Coast show on October 1. I finished my last stop in San Francisco and attended a press reception." She sits up straight and says, "I drove to Stanford Medical Center and checked myself in." The next day Ida had the surgery. Fortunately, the mass was benign and Ida was on her way to a full recovery. Quietly she says, "For an entire month I was very, very scared."

Ida pauses and says thoughtfully, "I came back to Microsoft a little too early." She had the surgery on October 2, but she had 165 people waiting for their job reviews to be in by November 1 in order to make the deadlines for reviews and bonuses—a very important process at Microsoft. Ida had taken three weeks off. "I went back, and of course there's no such thing as working a part-time schedule. All of my managers came to me with their reviews and we got them through. I went in to see Bill, who needed to approve the reviews. He had problems with some of the things I was doing. I had actually gone in to see about letting go someone that Bill had hired.

It just wasn't working, and nothing was going to move forward as long as this person was still in the organization. Bill and I got into it. I had this epiphany during that conversation. I thought, 'I did not go through what I just went through to be having this conversation! I did not survive for this!' I didn't blame Bill. Defending new salaries and bonuses requires some level of challenge and confrontation, but I didn't have the energy or the desire to continue as we had been doing."

Ida talked to Jon Shirley. "I needed to make a change," she says. "The company really wanted me to stay. I've always appreciated that. I had many choices as to what I could do. It was clear to me and to Bill that we just weren't working well together. We kept everything on hold for several months."

In 1985, Ida's division, Applications, was doing about $100 million in sales. At that time, Ida was working with some key products—Excel, Word, Project, and Chart. She says proudly, "The products came out on time, we had no attrition, and we had a happy organization. From that point of view, I was doing great at Microsoft, but I wasn't doing very well with Bill. He didn't know what he wanted me to be, and I wasn't very quick to pick that up."

Even though her relationship with Bill continued to falter, Ida made key improvements to the company. She says, "I did bring a different sense to the company. I brought a lot of organizational skills. I was, in fact, a more personable manager than many others had been. I had good groups working for me. For all the bluster at Microsoft, people rarely got fired. I came in and kind of cleaned house.

One of the things Ida noticed at both Apple and Microsoft was what she describes as a "raw environment." She says, "The common courtesies that are prevalent in almost every big company and professional environment were not present there. A lot of it had to do with how young everyone was. At Microsoft, the company was totally staffed by individuals who had been valedictorians of their class. They had won every contest they had ever entered. Now they were competing with each other. So you ended up with this strange machoism about how many hours you worked, how many days straight you were at the company, how many bugs you found in the software, and that sort of thing. It was a way to show that you were a competitor.

"In my career," Ida says, "I have never tried to be one of the boys. I am who I am and I take all of me into everything I do. I was older and from a different generation from Bill and Steve. They didn't consider me tough. But toughness is like Tupperware; there is a reason we don't eat off it every day just because it can bounce off the floor and won't break. There's nothing desirable about toughness by itself, and much less so by using it as a standard for evaluation. The truth is, I was as tough as anybody was. But I acted differently.

"Bill and I got along quite well during the time that Microsoft went public. They needed me as a VP of Applications—it was too big a part of the company to have in limbo or flux. When the company went public in March 1986, I went on the road show. I continued as VP of Applications during the initial public offering of Microsoft stock. It was an exciting time and a real honor to represent the applications business to the securities analysts in preparation for the public offering."

In May, Ida went to International, first as a director of International Products and later as the director of Marketing. Ida says, "I loved that job. It was a joy. I really loved it when I had a chance to step back and work with

Bill through someone else." Originally, Ida worked for Scott Oki, but Scott soon became senior VP of U.S. Domestic Sales. Then, Ida worked for Jeremy Butler, the new VP of International. "I had interviewed Jeremy when he came to Microsoft. I recommended him to be hired. I adored working for Jeremy. Jeremy did the entire interface with Bill except when I had to make a presentation. Bill and I got along great once that happened. Jeremy was very well respected in the company. With that level of respect, we always had what we needed to do the job in International."

International had a very different culture from Domestic. "It was almost a counterculture," Ida notes. "It was a small multinational group. We had lots of student interns who had come in to localize products, which involved, among other things, changing the product's language, screen appearance, units of measurement and currency, and packaging." Ida smiles and says, "They would always get themselves into trouble. I bailed a few of them out of jail. They didn't understand our culture. They didn't understand the concept of sexual harassment. They didn't understand many things. It was a huge challenge to get things done by people who were full-time but temporary and who had never worked in our culture. They were often from very wealthy families. They didn't know how to do their own laundry or get a driver's license. Jeremy always told me he could never run my group, but I had a ball, and we got so much accomplished. I loved the group. I loved what we were doing. We were considered stepchildren at Microsoft, but I didn't mind because we were out of the line of fire."

Ida and her group were doing adaptation of products. They came up with good cost guidelines for what it would cost to do a localized version of a product. Ida recalls their

Microsoft in 1978, when there were fewer than a dozen employees. **Bob O'Rear** is in the middle row, far left. Pictured (top to bottom, left to right) are Steve Wood, Bob Wallace, Jim Lane, Bob O'Rear, Bob Greenburg, Marc McDonald, Gordon Letwin, Bill Gates, Andrea Lewis, Marla Wood, and Paul Allen. *(Photo courtesy of Bob O'Rear)*

The early 1980s: **Scott Oki** is in the center. Also pictured (left to right, top to bottom) are Rowland Hanson, Jim Harris, Nahum Stiskin, Scott Oki, Mark Rolsing, John Shirley, Bill Gates, and Steve Ballmer. *(Photo courtesy of Scott Oki)*

Bob O'Rear, "The Mathematician," 1998. *(Photo courtesy of Bob O'Rear)*

Scott Oki, "The Force," c. 1990 with Windows 3.0. *(Photo courtesy of Microsoft Corp.)*

Min Yee, "Min," c. 1986. *(Photo courtesy of Min Yee)*

Ron Harding, "The Techie," 1999. *(Photo courtesy of Ron Harding)*

Dave Neir, "The CPA," 1989. *(Photo courtesy of Microsoft Corp.)*

Ida Cole, "The Independent," 1998. *(Photo courtesy of Ida Cole)*

Richard Brodie, "The Dilettante," Microsoft Christmas party, 1984. *(Photo courtesy of Richard Brodie)*

Russell Borland, "The Author," 1995. *(Photo courtesy of Russell Borland)*

Neil Evans, "The Professor," 1989. *(Photo courtesy of Microsoft Corp.)*

Scott Oki and Bill Gates, late 1980s. *(Photo courtesy of Microsoft Corp.)*

Paul Sribhibhadh, "The Diplomat," 1990. *(Photo courtesy of Paul Sribhibhadh)*

Min Yee shoving a pie in Bill Gates's face for a charitable event in 1989. Min paid $2,000 for the "privilege." *(Photo courtesy of Min Yee)*

Russell Steele, "The Musician," 1999. *(Photo courtesy of Russell Steele)*

Trish Millines Dziko, "The Athlete." *(Photo courtesy of Microsoft Corp.)*

decision-making process. "We started making business decisions rather than making purely emotional decisions about what products were going to be localized. We systematized things so that we still had room to move. If we owed a country manager a favor, we could do that and manage to justify it. We got more done than I could ever imagine. Everybody thought we were just taking products and adapting them. That's why we were considered a stepchild of Microsoft. But we were really creating products. There's no such thing as simply taking a product and making an international version. We had all the joy of creation. We were creating new products, new packaging, and new marketing strategies to put our products out. It was like a great development job, but without the politics."

Ida started the first development group outside of the United States. The group did product localization in Ireland, and Ida worked closely with the Irish government. She says, "We got quite a bit of grant money from them. I staffed the group and ran it. Now it's huge—it provides Europe with all of Microsoft products." The process used at Microsoft to get foreign products out at the same time as the U.S. products began when Ida was there. "We could put out one English-language product that could be sold in England, Australia, and Canada, so we didn't need to have two separate English-language products. We did other things to get out the French and German versions concurrently. Our goal was to get them out within thirty days after the U.S. version to prevent gray marketing. It was amazing! We got out secondary languages within sixty days."

International flourished while Ida was there, going from 32 products to 400 product releases a year during her tenure. Ida says, "We built an organization. We built a business. When I got there, International software business was very, very small. When I left in 1990, we were at $1 billion in sales, which represented around fifty-five percent of the company's revenue that particular year.

"I enjoyed my tenure at Microsoft so much," Ida says. "I do wish I had fared better early on. The company was very good to me and provided me a platform for everything I have done since. I really have to hand it to Bill and his direct staff at that time: Jon Shirley, Steve Ballmer, the late Jim Harris, and the late Frank Gaudette. The true problem-solving staff at Microsoft was just so good. It was the best-run company I have ever worked for. The company has made some very strong and good decisions."

Ida is forthright in her discussion of women in business, particularly at the executive level. "I believe in recognizing and nurturing talent in young people, regardless of their gender. I don't ever single out just women. Never! It separates women rather than integrates them. I talk to young people." Just because she was the first senior female executive at Microsoft, Ida doesn't feel she set a standard for women. "I reject that whole concept," she says vehemently. "It's not a valid concept. Competence to do a job is not a gender-related issue. It diminishes women rather than empowers them. All people have challenges that face them in the workplace when people who are not like them dominate it. I never participate in women's groups."

At Microsoft, Ida recognized and promoted several women who were talented. But Ida wants to be very clear on this issue. "*I didn't promote them because they were women.* They were the most talented candidates for the jobs available at the time. I'm glad that many of them went on to assume more responsibility at Microsoft and that their careers have been rewarding and successful."

Microsoft usually hired young people straight out of college, which is one of the reasons the company has succeeded. Ida observes, "They were all very young, fast moving, and in some ways apolitical. Even though they didn't always have many social skills, they were really sweet, but not very polished. I really cared about them. They were learning how to work in a Microsoft environment. Because they didn't have a lot of experience in other companies, they were easily shaped to work in the environment at Microsoft."

Ida was one of the few people to work both at Apple in its heyday and at Microsoft as it climbed to the top of the industry. "At Apple," she says, "there was an evangelical zeal. Microsoft was more of a grind-it-out kind of place. But at both places you had people who believed in what they were doing. They were led by the most brilliant minds of our time: Bill Gates and Steve Jobs. Despite our initial problems, I've always considered it a great privilege to work with someone like Bill who's doing it right and is thinking it out. Lots of people have sizzle and no steak—not Bill; he's the real thing. Steve Jobs has great flair. Bill is more methodical. He really goes through everything in order to get to an end point. Steve is more apt to create a gestalt where things become clear after you spend some time in that new space." Ida pauses. "They are two very different people."

Ida brings passion into every endeavor. "I've always thought that a balanced life denotes a lack of passion," she says. "I've never led a balanced life. I've never wanted to. For example, the idea of settling down with a nice man just doesn't interest me. Some people work for their families. That's their passion. It all has to do with tilting your life towards where your talent and interest take you. That's what young people should go after.

"As a high-level person in any organization, you have to be able to cope and have stamina—a lot will be thrown at you. You need to be able to perform no matter what the corporate politics are. You need the stamina to be standing at the end of the game. I see coping and stamina as being my most valuable traits in being able to succeed in business. I was always motivated by accomplishment and achievement."

But by 1990, Ida had been on the Apple and Microsoft fast track for more than 16 years. She was tired. "A new element came to Microsoft at that time. I was too spoiled to change." The new element brought with it more bureaucracy and red tape. It was more difficult to get things done. The company had grown, and a different approach was needed for its continued success. It was not a question of changing jobs or careers. "I retired," says Ida with emphasis. "But I'd do my Microsoft experience all over again."

Life after Microsoft

Ida Cole was responsible for saving one of Seattle's premier landmarks, the Paramount Theater, from the wrecking ball. After her retirement, a friend told Ida that the theater was in jeopardy. Along the way to renovating that historic landmark, Ida faced many hurdles. Initially, she and Frank Gaudette were partners, but Frank became too ill to participate. Many of Ida's Microsoft colleagues, along with other concerned Seattle residents, put up money to save the building. Those funds, along with grants from King County and the State of Washington, allowed the building to be purchased and renovated.

She overcame a number of financial hurdles raised by the city, and the Paramount Theater now hosts successful Broadway touring productions, such as *Ragtime* and *Miss Saigon*, as well as concerts and other live performances. The theater presented more than 250 events during 1998–1999.

Ida is a grandmother. "Being a grandmother is the best! My grandson's the apple of my eye." She always knew she'd be successful, but she says, "I didn't know *this* was coming my way!"

MIN YEE

"Min"

———■———

Microsoft: 1985–1992

Publisher, Microsoft Press, 1985–1992

Chairman, Microsoft's International Conference
on CD-ROM and Multimedia, 1986–1991

General Manager, Later Vice President, CD
Consumer and Multimedia, 1986–1992

MIN YEE

"Min"

The phrase "larger than life" is often overused, but it is hard to imagine anyone more aptly described by it than Min Yee. Rich in life experience, generous in spirit, almost omnivorous in intellectual curiosity, and physically imposing in stature, Min simply doesn't do things in a small way. He would be a man of rare flamboyance in any age or setting, the very antithesis of a button-down corporate executive.

For our interviews, he dresses in long-sleeved cotton shirts and slacks with suspenders. Early adversity taught Min Yee to take joy in life, and that joy is evident in his personal demeanor. He recounts his life's experiences—from his early childhood in an orphanage to his adventures as a freelance writer in the 1960s to his days as Microsoft corporate empire builder—in a gravelly voice, often punctuated by explosive bursts of deep-bellied laughter.

Through Min's energetic and inspired leadership, Microsoft Press was transformed from an unprofitable backwater of the company to a division at the very forefront of the communications technology breakthrough of the 1980s: CD-ROM and multimedia. Min was one of the first people to grasp the possibilities of the new medium and turn those possibilities into best-selling products. He developed Microsoft's first multimedia title, the Microsoft Multimedia Encyclopedia (code-named Merlin and later called Encarta) and eventually spawned an entire line of innovative multimedia applications, including a movie guide, an atlas, and a reference library. He took a book publishing department on the brink of financial collapse to one of the top per capita earning divisions of the company. Along the way, he inspired a generation of young men and women who went on to successful careers within Microsoft and beyond.

His unique style and prodigious accomplishments made him one of only a handful of people known throughout Microsoft by a single name: "Min."

The Path to Microsoft

After his mother died when he was 9, until the age of 15, Min Yee lived in an orphanage. His heritage includes Comanche Indian, Chinese, and Irish, and he learned firsthand the meaning of prejudice. He says, "I was *keenly* aware that I was not white. Parents told their daughters not to date me. I thought about being a lawyer, but there were 25,000 white lawyers. I just thought being a nonwhite in that environment would be too hard." Min's minister, John Gates (no relation to Bill), who adopted Min from the orphanage when the boy was 15, tried to protect him by offering what seemed to Min to be old, worn-out advice. "He told me not to get into a big, competitive work environment where my race would hold me back." At school, Min's teachers thought he could be successful, but Min didn't agree with them. He was learning some important life lessons. "I was at the orphanage in what seemed like an evolutionary survival battle among eighty kids. There were some hard lessons in learning how to survive and to cope with the world and understand how it really works."

Min later attended Denison University and graduated in 1960. He also attended Columbia University, where he majored in contemporary Chinese studies. At both schools, Min wrote for or edited the school newspapers and newsletters.

In the early 1960s, while attending Columbia, Min decided that the only way he could become truly proficient in the Chinese language was to travel to Taiwan and attend National Taiwan University in Taipei, because China was closed to American travelers. Min says, "I disembarked off a freighter in Keelung, Taiwan, with a wife, a baby, and seventeen dollars in my pocket." To pay for his studies, Min taught high school English and American history and wrote columns for the English-language newspaper. During that time, Time-Life News Service was hiring, and Min took a job as a reporter. He traveled around Asia by freighter, single-engine prop planes, motorcycles, and Chinese junk. "I've always been interested in geography and am kind of a map freak. I've always looked at a map and just wanted to dive right in, be at the longitude and latitude that appeared interesting. These days, we can really enjoy this as an armchair experience by drilling down on multimedia map programs. I thoroughly enjoyed that job in Asia."

Min's life was taking on its larger-than-life reputation, and, in addition to tragedy, he came face-to-face with danger. While Min was working as a foreign correspondent for Time-Life, his plane crash-landed in Danang, Vietnam. When they got out of the plane, Min said to the others, "Let's go get a drink!" Min recalls, "We were drunk for three days." Three weeks later, Min was staying in a Hong Kong hotel and woke up one morning paralyzed from the waist down. "I was like that for four hours until I could get a doctor to come to the hotel. It turned out to be delayed shock from the trauma of the airplane crash. The doctor gave me a bunch of shots, and I could feel the life coming back into my waist and legs. I was worried I was going to be paralyzed for the rest of my life."

Tragedy struck Min's family while he was away on assignment. His two-year-old son drowned in a fishpond while in the care of a nanny. As he and his wife tried to put the tragedy behind them, they had difficulty in conceiving another child. They adopted a baby girl whose twin sister had died. The family returned to the United States, where Time-Life helped Min secure a reporting job at the *Patriot Ledger* in Quincy, Massachusetts. But tragedy struck yet again. This time, Min's wife, who had been suffering from emotional and mental problems, died suddenly while being taken to a hospital.

Min remembers grappling with these horrendous tragedies: "Helene and I were just such an idealized couple, known by everybody. It seemed to me that something got screwed up in my mind—I didn't want to marry someone who hadn't known Helene. Everyone talked about her, the beautiful Unitarian, Jewish dancer. It seemed that anyone I dated would wonder and ask about her. They'd feel this big gap in my history, a gap that I really didn't want to talk about. So, at different times, I married three of her friends." It would take Min many years and five marriages until he again found happiness.

For the next 10 years, Min worked as a reporter for such noteworthy publications as the *New York Times*, the *Washington Post*, the *Boston Globe*, and *Newsweek*. While he was with *Newsweek*, he first reported on the aerospace industry and later on the Los Angeles sports scene and the Hollywood scene. He wrote articles on O.J. Simpson, Wilt Chamberlain, Goldie Hawn (who went to a rival high school) and the *Laugh-In* cast, and Raymond Burr. He became good friends with Burr and even wrote speeches for the *Perry Mason* and *Ironside* star. Burr, for his part, would cook for the young Yee family and play with Min's baby son, Tai. Other famous friends included Joni Mitchell, the Smothers Brothers, and the Mamas and Papas. He was invited to the Grammy and Academy Awards. "My wife Marcia and I would attend the Academy Awards and pull up in our little green Volkswagen Bug in between all the limos." Min also reported on the Manson murders in southern California: "On a Saturday morning in August, when I was on call for weekend duty, we were playing poker when a news editor in New York called me and told me to go cover some murders. I didn't know what a big story this would turn out to be, so I said, 'Hey, I'm in a killer poker game here and I've got a good hand. Are you sure you want weekend coverage on this?'" Min recalls the incident. "I called my photographer, chartered a helicopter, and flew over the estate where the bodies were lying on the ground. The cops kept waving up to us to get us to leave. But we got exclusive photography. In fact, my photographer, Dee Gorton, would gleefully yell over the *thwack-thwack* of the helicopter blades, 'This roll's for *Newsweek*, this roll's for *Paris-Match*. . . .' As it turned out, we had to cover that story round the clock and were dictating copy to the printers in Dayton just as the *Newsweek* presses started rolling early Sunday morning."

In 1969, while Min was still at *Newsweek* he was transferred from Los Angeles to San Francisco and wrote about racism and the Black Panther movement in California's prisons, which was just beginning. He started following the story after Fay Stender, a radical Berkeley attorney, came to the *Newsweek* offices to talk about the harsh prison conditions. By an arrangement with the California State Democratic Caucus, Min went undercover in Soledad to investigate these alleged conditions, at a pay of $1 per month. He was not, however, truly "undercover." At least the black prison inmates somehow knew (probably told by their attorney) that he was coming and set about quickly to protect him. Suspicious that white prisoners also knew and might want Min killed (subsequently blaming the black prisoners), the African-American inmates stuffed *Life* and *Look* magazines under his shirt as armor and accompanied him almost in a phalanx wherever he went.

Fay Stender's client was George Jackson, the author of *Prison Letters*, who was later shot to death at San Quentin during either an abortive uprising, a prison escape, or an execution setup, depending on whom you believe. George's younger brother Jonathan was one of the principals who took part in the Marin County courthouse tragedy in which he, other prisoners, and a judge were shot and killed. The judge had a shotgun taped to his mouth, which later discharged. Says Min of his jailhouse days, "When I got out, I wrote my report, but I also wanted to write a book about it." Min left *Newsweek* to write *The Melancholy History of Soledad Prison*. "I should have stayed at *Newsweek* and written the book at the same time," Min says. "It took longer than I thought and I ran out of advance money. I ended up living on food stamps. God, we hated going for the food stamps. The book was successful in terms of reviews, but it was not a huge commercial success."

After that, Min wrote a reference book published by Bantam, *The Great Escape: A Source Book of Delights and Pleasures for the Mind and Body*, which proved more successful commercially. By 1977, Min was between books and unemployed when a friend suggested he call Chevron/Ortho, as it was starting an in-house publishing program for gardening books. Min was at this point eager for a regular paycheck, and remained employed there for eight years. He didn't abandon freelance writing, however, and wrote a book about Jonestown, *In My Father's House,* which was published in 1981.

By 1985, Min decided it was time to move on. He was in his office typing out his resume when a printer salesman friend walked in and asked him what he was doing. Min said eight years was enough and he wanted to try something else. The friend said that he knew somebody who could use Min. "He wouldn't tell me who it was," Min says, "but the next day I got a call from Microsoft and they invited me up for an interview. I was there one day and had eight interviews! I interviewed with Jon Shirley and Bill Gates. The most exciting interview was with Bill. It was supposed to last twenty minutes, but we talked for over an hour. We talked about new optical media technology and how you could put existing content on the computer. You could have pictures and sound and movies—whatever you wanted to have—all linked together. I had done three things that were of interest to Microsoft. I had done some of the first electronic page makeup systems in the industry in terms of putting a few books together. Ortho Books was highly profitable; some titles today are in their thirty-second printing. Also, at Ortho we had done a secret research project with IBM in which we created a multimedia gardening title that had movies and still pictures. We used a LaserDisc. Bill talked with me about CD-ROM technology. I was superexcited. Beyond that, even if I was not offered a job, as a former newsman, it was just great that I had an interview with Bill Gates." Min was offered a job.

Life at Microsoft

In May 1985, Min became the new publisher of Microsoft Press, which comprised 27 people. Min recalls his first impressions of Press. "What struck me was that no one at Press used computers to work on books. The editor in chief used a pencil. Another thing was that none of the printing was put out to bid. I was used to getting three bids based on three conditions: how fast the printer could do the job, the ability to control quality, and how much it was going to cost. I insisted that by July 1, the previous bids should be put on my desk to see why they had chosen a certain printer. The bids did not show up. On the day of the deadline, that person quit. The saddest part was that the salesman who had gotten the job through good salesmanship was one of my best friends, and he had recommended me to Microsoft. But I could not continue that buddy system. Press was losing money hand over fist."

When Jon Shirley hired Min to run Press, he gave Min two years to turn it around and make it profitable. Min says, "I came out of publishing and knew the economics. I tried to explain those things to the people at Press. Initially, they didn't believe that a lack of profitability was all that bad. At the first meeting, an editor asked rhetorically, 'Well, we sold some books, didn't we?' By the second meeting I had our controller from Finance join me in the meeting to explain the financial ABCs of book publishing. During all this time, I did not inform my colleagues that Press would be shut down if it was not profitable. I thought this would be too demoralizing and create too much anxiety. The best-selling title at the time was *Running MS-DOS* by Van Wolverton, a top seller for years. MS Press made a franchise out of the 'Running' titles: *Running Excel, Running Windows,* and other Running titles."

Min's favorite title is *Programmers at Work,* a series of interviews with the great programmers of the day talking about programming as a creative art form. "The idea was not new," Min said, "I actually stole it from Malcolm Cowley and George Plimpton, from the Writers at Work series, one of the treasure troves of American (primarily) literature." Among the pioneer programmers interviewed were Charles Simonyi (Multiplan and Word), John Warnock (Adobe's PostScript), Gary Kildall (CPM), Bill Gates (BASIC for PCs), C. Wayne Ratliff (dBASE III), Dan Bricklin (VisiCalc), Jonathan Sachs (Lotus 1-2-3), Ray Ozzie (VisiCalc and Lotus 1-2-3), Jef Raskin (the Apple MacIntosh computer), and Toru Iwatani (Pac Man).

In the beginning Press published books about the popular Lotus 1-2-3. "This would drive Scott Oki up the wall because he was in marketing and we were touting someone else's software. But Lotus (and this was before Excel shipped) had a huge installed base and we wanted to sell into that. Also, because of the pride we had as a publishing house, we didn't want to be a vanity press and only do books about our own products. The feeling was that books by other publishers about Microsoft products legitimized the products better than we could. For example, when we shipped Excel to combat Lotus, then the more books about Excel published by rival publishers helped to legitimize our product. So, even though we were part of Microsoft, we had to compete against other publishers. But we got the best writers so that our books were recognized and viewed in the industry as the best books written on the subjects. We didn't try to teach anybody how to use the products because that was the job of the manuals. The first year, we'd take the proposed book list and new titles to Bill for his approval. After about a year, he just let us do it. He had faith that we knew what titles should be done."

Another of Min's key achievements was the quality of books that Microsoft Press published. "We won a lot of awards from the Computer Press Association," says Min proudly. "And we were really very profitable, not as a software publisher would be profitable, but certainly among the top in trade book publishing.

"You can't say we were as profitable as the software side because they could charge double-digits for their products. But compared to other book publishers we were very profitable. That's the only way you can measure it. We had sales of more than $300,000 a year, per employee. That was higher than the per-employee revenue number for Microsoft as a whole."

Bill Gates trusted Min to run Press, and Min explains that trust. "I came out of the publishing world and knew publishing economics. My predecessor was really more of a start-up guy. Bill doesn't have much background in publishing and consumer products. His strength is in computers and technology. I could be the guy he could look to for publishing content titles. At heart, I am really a content guy, maybe with some storyteller in me. One of my hobbies is reference works; I collect them. Maybe that's why he listened to me about CD-ROM and multimedia titles. Maybe I just talked a good game."

In the world of technology, there are some who wonder why Bill Gates wanted to have his own press. Min says, "I think Bill has always been in love with books. Chris Banks, who was my senior director at Press, said it best. 'It's my understanding that when Bill sees a gap in something that is critical to the whole thing, he will try and fill that gap. That's the reason Microsoft got involved with hardware at one point. He might have seen books as a way to increase the consumer's comfort level with Microsoft products and help them use the products. It helped to get Microsoft's name out there in a respected way.' "

By the mid-1980s, technological developments in the computer field were opening new possibilities for creating compelling applications for business and home users. The introduction of CD-ROMs, with their massive storage capabilities, immediately struck Yee, Gates, and other top brass at Microsoft as an important opportunity. They began strategizing ways that Microsoft could assure itself a piece—and eventually a dominant piece—of the new multimedia industry.

Min was one of the executives given responsibility for formulating and implementing Microsoft's multimedia strategy. He set out organizing conferences, gathering resources, and publishing industry white papers and technical reviews to garner momentum and leadership for Microsoft's development efforts and to ensure that MS-DOS would be the main platform for any industry-wide multimedia initiative. Under his leadership, Microsoft began its first multimedia publishing ventures, creating a multimedia encyclopedia (Encarta), reference library (Bookshelf), movie guide (Cinemania), and other consumer applications that laid the groundwork for the CD-ROM/multimedia computing explosion of the 1990s.

Min recalls, "Every Sunday afternoon during the summer of 1985, three of us (Raleigh Roark, Rob Glaser, and I) would gather to meet with Bill in his office to discuss a content-driven technology that would revolutionize personal computing. This technology was CD-ROM and its ability, eventually, to deliver content in text, photos, sound, and video. We knew that there would be an immense future in this, and Bill was aware early that Microsoft needed to license or own, preferably own, a vast amount of content. One of each of our weekly chores in preparation for this meeting was to continually prepare and update a list of what we called 'the Vanilla Top Twenty,' a list of the twenty most promising generic multimedia titles that would have broad consumer appeal. Leading off my list were such titles as Microsoft Multimedia Encyclopedia (later Encarta), Microsoft Writing and Editing Tools, a set of books that I kept handy as a writer and editor like *The Chicago Manual of Style, Webster's Third International, Bartlett's Quotations, Roget's Thesaurus*, the *Columbia Encyclopedia*, an atlas, and a biographical dictionary (this later became Microsoft Bookshelf), Microsoft's Movie Review Database (later Cinemania), an AMA Medical Guide to Personal Health, a Microsoft Multimedia Atlas (inspired by Charles and Ray Eames's *Powers of Ten*), beginning with a spinning globe whereby a user could 'drill down' to road maps, train or plane schedules, or even a video of the Great Wall of China.

"One Saturday, Gary Kildall was in Seattle and spent the afternoon on Bill G's boat. Gary was doing pioneer work evangelizing the virtues of CD-ROM to the corporate world and complained that it would take him almost an entire day just to explain the technology to potential content providers and users. Gary said he was frustrated and losing a great deal of time and money in conducting such exercises. After Bill related this conversation to us at our Sunday meeting, I immediately suggested that we (Microsoft) host the first of a series of conferences and seminars on CD-ROM. We would not try to profit monetarily from such a conference, but as a preemptive move it would push us to the industry forefront in leading the world into CD-ROM, making certain that CD-ROM ran under an MS-DOS operating system. Bill immediately gave me a budget and said, 'Do it.' I was de facto drafted to serve as chairman of 'Microsoft's International Conference of CD-ROM' with the tag line '. . . and Multimedia' later added."

Three weeks before the first conference was held at the

Sheraton Hotel in Seattle, Min recalls, "It looked like there were about eight hundred people who wanted to speak (that is, fly in free and attend gratis) and about eighty who were willing to pay to attend. We charged close to $1,000 per head because it's not cheap to put on a conference. We didn't want to do cheap food either. At one conference we flew in 25,000 pounds of tiger shrimp from Singapore. We became known as the conference that never ran out of shrimp. Of course, we had a lot of fine food, but the comments were focused on shrimp." By the time the conference started, 1,000 people attended. "It put Microsoft in the forefront of leading CD-ROM and multimedia development," says Min. "We were *the* conference, and we got to choose the keynote speaker. I thought that having Bill Gates and Gary Kildall speak at the first conference would be both historically interesting and bring to closure, at least emotionally, the gap between the CPM and MS-DOS platforms. Here were the two owners of those platforms and they were coming together to support CD-ROM technology.

"After that, since we owned the show, we always considered our keynote speakers carefully. If they didn't run DOS, 'Pimp 'em!,' as Bill would say. If you don't have standards, you have confusion. We wanted the standard to be the things Microsoft was working on. If we used somebody else's standard, then we'd have to change everything. We wanted people to sign on with a standard we were comfortable with. For us, that standard was called MS-DOS." Min considers the technology conferences one of his key achievements at Microsoft.

"Once we got to a point beyond being restricted to CD-ROM hypertext, we got into developing proposals to sign up various computer manufacturers to build a machine that would be capable of running content in various media formats. We mulled over such names as OPC [Optical Personal Computer], HPC [Home Personal Computer] and MPC [Multimedia Personal Computer]. I came down heavy in favor of calling the new machines 'MPC,' and our multimedia systems evangelists were charged with signing up software and hardware vendors to make their machines and software 'Microsoft MPC–compliant.'

"Initially, it was extremely difficult for us to sign up content providers. In trying to buy the rights to *Britannica*, its CEO Peter Lynch said to me that if Microsoft placed the entire contents of the encyclopedia on one CD-ROM disc and sold it he'd lose *Britannica's* most important asset. Then, rhetorically, Lynch asked me if I knew what his most important asset was, and promptly told me it was his great sales force: If his sales force thought they would be competing against the sale of a single disc, they'd leave and go sell cars or soap. We never did license from *EB*, but we did the next best thing: I hired two of *EB's* top editors to join Microsoft. I tried to hire Mike Reed, *EB's* managing editor, but although he did not join us, we remained friends. Bill even wrote the personal computer article entry in the new *Britannica*, which Tom Corddry actually first drafted for Bill G's input and rewrite, and I edited.

"Eventually, the drive to secure content led me to visit with numerous content providers to license their content or to purchase their companies: Hammond's (atlas, for Bookshelf); HarperCollins (reference division, no deal in purchasing the division but we did make several licensing agreements, including the audio rights to readings by Dylan Thomas, Robert Frost, T. S. Eliot, etc., for Bookshelf); Bartholomew's (atlases, no deal); Funk & Wagnall's (licensed text for twenty-one years with rights to edit, add, or otherwise change, credit to be in very fine print. Although Bill wanted rights 'in perpetuity,' our lawyers said that was illegal); *World Book Encyclopedia* (no deal, but I did hire their president, Peter Mollman, for Microsoft); *Bettmann Archives* (no deal initially); the *Columbia Encyclopedia* from Columbia University Press (they felt they were selling their 'family jewels,' but I hired away their negotiator); McGraw-Hill (no deal for their professional reference works); Houghton-Mifflin (*American Heritage Dictionary*); Dorling Kindersley (purchased 26 percent of the company and electronic rights to all text and art); Hulton Photo Archives (deal made); the San Francisco Exploratorium (and the name 'Exploratorium'); the Smithsonian collection; *Larousse Encyclopedia;* the *AMA Medical Encyclopedia; Mayo Clinic Encyclopedia* (when the AMA deal fell through). At the same time, we also approached media giants like The New York Times, ABC, and CBS, trying to license video and scripts to include in products on future, more robust platforms. You would be able to call up anything from 'Danang 1968' to 'Picasso's studio' to taking a tour of the British Museum or walk atop the Great Wall of China. It would all be information at our fingertips."

It was Min's responsibility to find an encyclopedia that would license the rights for the content to be put onto CD-ROM. Finally, the publishers of *Funk & Wagnall's,* sold in grocery stores for $3 a volume, agreed to license the content of their encyclopedia to Microsoft for 21 years. "Bill wanted to license it in perpetuity, but we found out that was illegal," Min says. "*Funk & Wagnall's* was actually well reviewed in sources that did serious reviews of encyclopedias. It wasn't a piece of trash. We wanted the right to add to it and rewrite anything. We wanted to build up its timeliness and coverage."

Min and his staff worked on the interface of Encarta, for which there was no precedent. "We had to solve problems as to how to filter the information—did you do it by date and by search? How would you find things easily, quickly, and have it come on the screen and be meaning-ful? How would the screen look? Where do you put the navigation buttons? On the top? On the side? On the bottom? In more than one place? Remember, this was among the first attempts at reference navigation, before everyone became used to Internet browsers, with their attendant top navigation bars, and frame filters."

Min worked primarily on programming the interface and creating the architecture of the information the disc would contain. Today, such activity would be called "information architecture," and "content management."

Today, many people can claim some kind of credit for the early work on the first Encarta. Tom Corddry (project management, interface, and information architecture), Carolyn Bjerke (designer), Alan Hartman (programmer and production), and Min worked on the interface; Ed Kelly and Min concentrated on all the acquisitions neces-sary, including those for Bookshelf and Cinemania. The editorial base was senior editor Pat Combs (hired away from Britannica) and Bob Phillips (hired away from Funk & Wagnall's), while Stephen Brown concentrated on audio production. Nils Von Veh had perhaps the toughest job: He was responsible for developing the business case back-grounder for Gates's approval as well as the marketing plan for Encarta's first rollout. Finally, Craig Bartholomew was brought in from Bookshelf marketing to manage the encyclopedia project on a day-to-day basis. Craig, to this day, is the general manager of Microsoft Learning—he's been called the "Encarta Baron."

"When thinking about the early Merlin days," recalled Min, "people forget, after something like that has been so successful, just how uncertain its fate was in the early days. When we were trying to get Encarta figured out, we had a devil of a time attracting decent developers from elsewhere in the company, so we got great work out of such 'rebels' as Dan Newell, who in turn got code written by interns like Kevin Gammill and Phil Spencer. Many of the early contributors were certainly not 'mainstream' types, but pioneers and oddballs. . . . Pradeep Singh was not exactly your center-cut junior woodchuck MBA, for example, any more than Tom Corddry or Susan Lammers or I was very 'normal' by Microsoft standards. Many of us went nuts or went out the door in later years when the thing got big and the mainstream personalities took over."

According to his staff, one of Min's biggest contributions was that he stood up for what they were doing at the highest levels, at a time when many of the executive staff and many on the board thought Bill was wasting his time and their money mucking around with multimedia.

Every three weeks they'd take a new interface version to Bill, and he'd ask questions and tell them what he liked and what he didn't like. Min says, "We had to have his okay. Normally, Bill wants to okay everything and ride tight until he thinks you've got it. Then he doesn't worry about it."

The next problem for Min and his staff was how to illustrate Encarta. "We thought about buying Bettmann Archive [a company with 16 million photographs, now wholly owned by Gates], the British publisher Dorling Kindersley. DK had about 30,000 pieces of art, and The Hulton Deutsch Collection, which had 15 million photographs, prints, and engravings. Bill was keenly interested in also having those rights for his other company, Continuum, which was later called Corbis." Bill might not have purchased these companies if it were not for Min's suggestion that he do so.

During the Microsoft board meeting to consider the Dorling Kindersley purchase, Min had 30 multimedia titles mocked up, printed, and inserted in blank jewel cases—the exact equivalent of blads in publishing—and dumped them out in a big pile on the conference table. "Bill's eyes just locked in on that pile. He wanted that pile to be real. Bill laughed when I emptied them out of a shopping bag, but he spent the rest of the meeting fending off the skeptics on the board, and got the green light to do the deal. It was great theater."

But the board's view was that a $26 million investment in DK also meant an additional $600 million needed to develop products from the acquisition. That led to the beginning of what Min called the phantom phase of the multimedia encyclopedia, because Jon Shirley wanted Min to promise that the Merlin team would cease work on the encyclopedia so that financial resources could be applied to the development of DK titles. Min said he would.

"Bill officially agreed to kill the encyclopedia project so we could devote all our time to doing DK-based titles," Min recalled. "Of course, DK had no intention of cooperating in that, as we slowly learned. DK had its own agenda, which was more like learning Microsoft's multimedia programming technology and marketing strategies to build their own titles." Min sensed this and did not really trust the relationship. A few years later, DK went public and Microsoft sold its share, clearing something like $90 million on the original $26 million investment that Min had convinced the Microsoft board to make.

"We never quit the encyclopedia design work, but we were otherwise dead in the water until Craig and Tom Ikeda proposed creating 'Bookshelf Encyclopedia,' which immediately put the encyclopedia team back in business. I believe Bill wanted us to do it, but needed to be able to keep his promise, technically, to the board," said Min.

Essentially, Min lied to the board to keep the multimedia project alive. "I had no real intention of stopping work on Merlin," Min said. "I had to lie, if you want to call it that: It was a risk I had to take. We had sunk too many resources into the project and I knew that it would bring great returns. I knew that we would end up doing a great job." Today, the encyclopedia sells approximately 8 million copies a year, 1 million of these in foreign languages. It outsells all other encyclopedias—print and disc—combined.

When Min started work on the encyclopedia, the shipping version of Windows was 2.1 ("shipping" being a euphemism because nobody was buying it—they were still all using DOS), so the design team had to work with only a sketchy idea of what Win 3 was going to look like or be able to do. The majority of PCs at that point were 286's; the 640K RAM limit was still the norm; 20-meg hard drives were typical; and sound cards were rare.

Min was one of the few male bosses at Microsoft who promoted women. Min says, "It was all about brains, work speed, and dedication. Being a woman had nothing to do with it. It just so happened that many of the best employees we had at Press that had those qualities were women. One woman whom I promoted on a regular basis was Susan Lammers, who began working with me at Chevron/Ortho and whom I recruited to come to Microsoft. During her first few months at Chevron, Susan only worked a few hours a day and spent the rest of the time reading fiction and nonfiction. Her colleagues complained to me about this. Upon checking it out, I discovered that Susan was finishing everything—editing, rewriting, hiring and assigning stylists and photographers, and working with our designers—that was her job and had time left over. It turned out that she was happy to be assigned more work." Eventually, Bill Gates hired Susan away from Press and Multimedia to run his Interactive Home Systems, which became Continuum and, later, Corbis.

She's now the CEO of the successful Headbone Interactive. Min also hired and promoted Patty Stonesifer, who became senior VP; she and Ida Cole were the two most successful women at Microsoft. "Patty personified the ideal manager because she was understanding, articulate, and smart. She was a great manager. She could hobnob with anybody. She was terrific at marketing and handling people. When I started managing Multimedia, I hired her to run Press. I didn't give up my title, though, because I liked being a publisher, but she really ran things."

In 1985, one of the first CD-ROM multimedia projects Min came up with was Bookshelf, a reference title. For Min, a writer by background, it was important to have a small shelf of reference books that were in close proximity as tools of the writer. "I was in charge of Compact Disc–Interactive, or CD-I, so named for the Phillips technology. For a while, we were changing names, it seemed, by the fiscal quarter. Soon we were called CD Consumer."

During Min's travels seeking multimedia advice and alliances, he met Tom Lopez, the CEO of a small start-up called Citation. It turned out that Lopez had already been working on a Bookshelf-like product. Min brought Lopez aboard as a consultant and was keen for Bill to meet him. For Min, Lopez seemed a great asset for Microsoft to pursue. Lopez was what Min wasn't: a button-down type. Eventually, Bill hired Lopez and formed a CD-ROM business group, headed by Lopez.

"We thought of Tom's group as the business multimedia group and our group as the information/consumer group. We were doing the encyclopedias and Cinemania, while Tom was charged with coming up with business applications. 'You get to have all the fun,' Tom said to me once. He was right."

As a cineast, one of Min's dream products was to build

a movie encyclopedia. From the specifications that he wrote out in the summer of 1985, he envisioned a product that included all the reviews by Pauline Kael, Leonard Maltin, Peter Travers, even James Agee; profiles of directors, writers, cinematographers, film editors, and actors; and, of course, sample dialogue and motion video of significant scenes from selected films. Today, 14 years later, all of this is available on-line.

Turf wars ensued between the two groups, as their work often overlapped. "When Lopez left the company and his group got folded into ours, some guys gave me high fives as if we'd won something. But it wasn't a competition between Tom and me. We really worked in different worlds. Some competition would have been good, but we were both so new that we didn't need to compete for resources or for Bill's attention. Bill was always interested in both groups. I think the feeling was far more competitive at the technical programming level, not the content level. There was a huge competition that's still going on today. To me, that's the supernegative side of Microsoft. A competitive spirit is great, but not at the expense of killing someone's else spirit. It seemed like the tech people just have a different mind-set. The consumer people are far more well rounded and more humanities oriented."

Min was always pushing Bill to do new and different titles. "I convinced Bill that we should do a line of books called Tempus, meaning both 'timeliness' and 'timelessness.' I like to think I sold Bill on the idea by saying, 'The symbol is going to be an hourglass, just like the waiting hourglass in Windows.' That was a bit naive on my part, but he agreed to let us give it a try. We had some success with it and did some good books in terms of the quality of the content." The subject areas of Tempus Books were in general science, mathematics, philosophy, and chess.

While at Microsoft Press, Min reported to Jon Shirley, the president. "He's a great man. He is blessed with a keen no-nonsense business mind." Min's favorite quote of Jon Shirley's occurred when Jon was asked by *Fortune* magazine why he chose Goldman Sachs to handle Microsoft's IPO. "Jon said, matter-of-factly, 'Better the whore you know than the whore you don't.' "

Although Min reported to Jon, Bill Gates wanted to know directly what was going on in Multimedia. "To meet with Bill, you had to prepare for about three weeks! You had to worry about covering all the questions that he might ask—he picks up on everything so fast. You can't hand him anything to read because then you have nothing to talk about. You hand him the written stuff after you talk to him because he will stay ahead of you the whole time. If certain points are weak, he is going to see right through them and attack. He's extremely brilliant."

On a trip to Radio Shack headquarters in Dallas, Min saw another side to Bill. "He was talking a mile a minute on the phone. It turned out we were on the same flight coming back. Bill was so intensely into his conversation that he was totally oblivious to the impending flight departure. I felt like it was kind of my responsibility to make sure he got on the plane. He's kind of a kid in a way—he doesn't keep in mind that the damn plane might take off without him! I was in first class. I always personally paid for the part of the fare to upgrade because of my bulk. Bill was back in coach where he normally is. He'll sit on an aisle seat, throw a blanket over his head and go to sleep. I asked him if he wanted to come up to first class after we took off. Bill came up to first class, looked around, and said, 'You know, this is pretty neat up here!' "

Patty Stonesifer spoke about Min and his management style. After being promoted to Microsoft's general manager of Canada she wrote a memo to her two direct reports (Chris Banks and Jim Brown) about Min's management style, because they would now be reporting to Min. She wrote:

Quick Reference Guide to Min Yee Management

A rambling guide to a happy working relationship
Dedicated to Chris Banks and Jim Brown
by
Patty Stonesifer

Min asked me to write down my "methods" for interacting with him, since we have reached a good "comfort level" working together the past two years—and he would like to have the same type relationship with you. First, let me say that these are not meant as "commands," by any means. Everyone communicates differently, this is simply the way I found worked best with me for Min.

90/5/5 Management Style
I heard it first this week from my NEW boss, but recognized it immediately as the same style Min employs. On 90% of your job, just do it without input. "He doesn't really want to know!" On 5% send him some "FYI" mail after you do it or copy him on a summary memo/report, so in case he gets involved/hears about it he can simply have absorbed enough to know where you're headed. On the last 5% get him involved directly—bring him the issues AND YOUR PROPOSED SOLUTION, and discuss it with him/get his input and feedback BEFORE you act. That means that less than 2 hours per week are necessary for direct contact. Most of that we have spent at the Yankee Diner, just going over "trends" and issues. (Okay, and eating pot roast, too.)

It is fairly obvious to you what needs to be in the 5/5

slots. The most important thing is you tell him about PROBLEMS, even if you have every belief that you will soon have them under control. If you do not want him to "act," then tell him so. But telling him that the problem exists is essential. He does not like to hear it first from someone else. Tell him about anyone who is hot and likely to get to him (staff, vendor, author, mgmt), any sales or expense variances, any deviation from the norm. Get his INPUT on any policy changes (like discount, etc.), major personnel changes, series, profit issues, anything affecting top line or bottom line performance.

On long range issues and "opportunities," take him to lunch, tap his thoughts, then let him know later where you are headed. I tease that I like to take Min's "pulse" at least once a day, but in a way I am serious. I like to stop in and just do a "quick check" on whether he has anything brewing—opportunities that trip over the transom (and on to his desk), requests for info, et ceteras. These "checks" take only about 2–3 minutes. I do them daily, and only once a week do they seem to turn into a "sit down" where I actually stay to review an issue that is important enough to warrant further exploration. But it helps Min keep a finger in the daily activity in Books.

Reports—Min likes 'em, I hate 'em. If you do them you get extra points—and it helps Press visibility outside of EastTech! The quarterly report is essential and was requested by Jon S [Jon Shirley]—so don't let that slide.

New General Manager—you may disagree with this, but I have recommended that Min seriously look for one. The principal reason has nothing to do with your replication of MY skills—since I am a "generalist" by nature, and as such easily replaced. Rather I suggested that Min look for a seasoned Trade/Education sr. manager who would bring additional channel experience (education, other), ideally have run the entire operation of a $40 million dollar publisher—knows a great deal about self-operated book distribution et cetera. In short, someone that EX-PANDS the skill set of the management team beyond the skills that I had, not someone who simply has "more" of what you and Suzanne and Jim already offer. He has assured me that he is in no hurry to run out and find a replacement, so you will have ample opportunity to influence his decision or change his direction. You have heard it from me so often that I'm sure it makes you choke—I am a firm believer that there IS more than one right way to run ANY organization. I am sure you will improve what we have already done. I only hope I have this kind of group in Canada.

It has been great working with you both. Thanks for all the help. Have fun!

By 1990, Min's health deteriorated. While in Hawaii with his fifth wife, "My health went to hell in a handbasket," Min says. "I was overweight, and my wife hated the Seattle area. I didn't know that I'd suffered a stroke until six months after it happened. My blood pressure was running 300/200. I remember one time I was supposed to give a speech with Bill at this gathering in New York. My blood pressure got so high that I had to fly back home. I couldn't handle it. I left the company about a year after that. The drugs that I took to control the blood pressure had a lot of side effects. I couldn't drive a car or walk down the halls without hitting a wall. I really couldn't do my job at that point."

He has succinct advice for young people in search of a career: "Find a great company and just get in the door." One of the reasons Min joined Microsoft was because he knew it was going to be a phenomenal success. "Microsoft had control of the heart of the information beast and Bill was willing to take chances. That was obvious. Before I worked there, I'd never been able to afford to buy any stock. When Microsoft came out with MS-DOS in 1981, I bought one of the first IBM PCs. About two months later I called Microsoft and asked them if they were selling any stock. Some woman there laughed at me and hung up. After I went to work for Microsoft, I was given stock options and the stock paid for itself." Min pauses to chuckle. "One of my former wives signed away any rights to my future earnings while we were going through a divorce. She didn't think I'd ever make any significant money!"

Min remembers his days at Microsoft as "a time gone by, a great time that has passed, but I feel that way about everywhere I've worked. It was all a great time. I've been fortunate in being able to work with wonderful, bright people and work on great, challenging products, especially on products in which I could learn something."

Life after Microsoft

"I needed more than a year to recover from the health problems I had when I left Microsoft before I could even consider working again," says Min. In 1993, Min accepted the position of vice president of Media Vision and established its multimedia development team in Bellevue, Washington. After leaving Media Vision in April 1994 because he disagreed with some of the company's business practices, Min started to create multimedia products and art books on his own. Min created The Great Cities of Europe for his company, CinéWorld, both as a CD-ROM and as an Internet-based tour of the great cities of Europe. "Working on this product was a joy, as it combined my love of travel with my love of art, reference, and education. I hope to expand it in the future to include other great cities of the world," says Min. He also oversaw the publication of *Yoshitoshi's One Hundred Aspects of the Moon.*

Currently involved in a biotech start-up company, Min has plans for creating future Internet sites, a return to writing, and consulting on multimedia products and Internet development. "I truly enjoy working in this industry. I find myself continually learning and sharing ideas with fine minds, young and old, who have chosen publishing as the professional world for their lives, whether that world is in books, on discs, or sailing across a telephone wire." With his health fully returned, Min keeps active indeed.

It was stated earlier in this chapter that it would take Min many years and five marriages until he again found happiness. During his last months at Microsoft, after his stroke in Hawaii and his drastic jump in blood pressure, Min was urged by his French tutor and another friend to attend a seminar on dying conducted by Stephen Levine, author of the best-selling book on death and dying, *Who Dies?*

At that seminar he met Dianne Quicker Dussault, and after talking with her for several hours, he could not get her out of his mind. At 6 A.M. the following morning, Min appeared at the office of his neurologist and told his doc-tor that he could not eat, sleep, or read—that he could only think of Dianne. He thought, Min said, that he must be deeply in love with this woman. The doctor asked, "How often does this feeling come over you? Once a year, once a month, a week, once a day?"

Min replied, "Only once in my lifetime."

The doctor said, "You'd better go marry her."

And he did.

RON HARDING

"The Techie"

Microsoft: 1986–1990

Technical Manager

Software Developer

Multimedia, Microsoft Press International,
Computer-Based Training Group

RON HARDING

"The Techie"

Ron Harding is tall, lanky, and fit. At 49, he is an avid hiker and travels the world in search of good trails. His voice is soft and whispery and his demeanor trusting. Although a multimedia tool he created is in the Smithsonian, he is reluctant to sing his own praises.

At Microsoft, Ron was an anomaly. He had expertise in software *and* hardware—two very different disciplines. As a result, he was often used as an interface between design and technical groups. During his years at the company, he worked as a technical manager and software developer in such diverse areas as the Computer-Based Training Group, Microsoft Press International, and the Multimedia Group.

Despite his many responsibilities, Ron was unusual in that he worked a 40-hour week. He was a Vietnam vet and more mature than many of the people he worked with. Although no less committed than his colleagues, his approach to work and life was different.

The Path to Microsoft

In the mid-1960s, Ron Harding enjoyed his job as an aeronautical draftsman at Boeing. He had gone through the government's Manpower Development program, where he learned the trade of aeronautical drafting and finished top in his class. When the Vietnam War came along, the United States government drafted Ron. Ron opted to join the Marines Corps because he thought it would be slightly safer. He was put into a special unit of amphibious tractors that were outfitted to clear mine-fields. It was a harrowing time. "We used to get shot at by artillery. It was very unnerving—especially during the Tet offensive. They shot at us early in the morning when the sun was coming up and was very bright. You couldn't see where the artillery was coming from. If you heard the shell, it had already gone off."

For 13 months, this was Ron's day-to-day existence. Toward the end of his duty, he became worried. He recalls the fear, but says quietly, "You wonder, 'Am I going to get shot? I've got a week left. Am I going to make it?' "

Ron survived. In 1966 he returned to Seattle and hooked up with his old high school friends. Despite the cultural conflict over the Vietnam War, he became part of the hippie scene. For several years he enjoyed that experience. He smiles and remembers a different time and place. "Everybody was so friendly—they would just take you in. We could hitchhike around the country and not feel worried about it. There was a trust that isn't here today. Even the drug scene was different—not as violent as it is now."

But Ron had always wanted to go to college, so in 1972 he entered Seattle Community College and two years later the University of Washington. He received his degree in math, specializing in numerical analysis.

At the University of Washington, Ron helped design and build computers that were used for monitoring medical research. He also helped develop the software. The computers were sold to other universities, and Ron often traveled throughout the United States to fix or update them. The National Institutes of Health funded the research. While at the university, Ron learned a great deal about hardware design and debugging. But after 10 years, he decided he wanted to live and work somewhere else.

Ron laughs and says, "I got as far as St. Louis." He took a position at Emerson Electric in its defense end. At the time, Emerson was developing an interactive videodisc system for the military that would take the place of the classroom training sessions. Ron says, "I stayed there about one and a half years, but I was carrying on a long-distance relationship so I quit and moved back to Seattle."

Ron took a job with a small start-up company called IXION. There were only three employees, and Ron was hired as a software developer. The company made interactive videodiscs. Ron says, "Their claim to fame was the CPR dummy that was developed for the American Heart Association. It was a pretty big hit and is still used."

While at IXION, Ron developed an interactive video system that was used to teach welding. He developed the hardware and software for the actual welding torch that was run across a TV screen. With quiet pride, Ron says, "It was a prototype that ended up in the Smithsonian. It was a really good teaching tool."

In 1986, Tom Lopez, the VP for the CD-ROM group at Microsoft, visited the company. Ron remembers that day. "They were looking at what we did. They'd done Bookshelf, but they wanted to do other things with CD-ROM. I'd heard about Microsoft when I was at Emerson, but my interests weren't piqued. In 1983, there were so many other little companies around."

By the time Ron was at IXION, he had taken serious note of Microsoft. By 1986, Microsoft stock had gone public and was doing very well due to the success of such products as, MS-DOS, Multiplan, Word, Windows, and Excel. "I considered taking out a second mortgage on my house to buy Microsoft stock, but I didn't do it." Ron chuckles at the memory.

Although Ron liked his job at IXION, it was a small company with little opportunity for advancement. Ron decided to apply at Microsoft.

Life at Microsoft

In December 1986, Microsoft Press International hired Ron as a technical manager. At the time, Press was very involved with CD-I technology (more specifically, Compact Disc-Interactive). CD-I is a standard for a form of optical disc technology that can combine audio, video, and text on a high-capacity compact disc. It has such features as image display and resolution, special effects, audio, and animation. The company worked with Philips and other companies, which were developing a stand-alone player that used a CD-ROM disc. Ron notes, "I was the CD-I technical manager; I had to be up on all the CDI technology. I would do all of the specifications. There was a sense at Press that CD-I was going to be very competitive with CD-ROM. Potentially, CD-I had much more to offer. It had everything: a computer and its own graphics. There was an interactive video system that was small, a little bigger than a laptop. They developed the whole system for the consumer market. It was much faster and had everything built into the player, as opposed to CD-ROM, which was just a drive attached to a computer." As Philips pushed the hardware technology, Ron and others waited and waited. "Press was thinking about an encyclopedia on CD-I, but the hardware kept getting delayed," says Ron. "We kept following it, but all we had were the specifications—no hardware. It was my job to do all of those specifications."

After a year, the group realized CD-I was not going to work out. "Philips came out with the hardware just recently, within the last few years," Ron says. "Even though CD-I could have been very competitive with CD-ROM, we had to cover all our bases and work on different things. If you're developing applications, then you have to develop them for hardware that has a market share. If there was a computer with market potential, we'd write software for it," Ron points out.

At Press, Ron turned his attention to CD-ROM technology. It was a new technology and very slow in data transfer, which made it difficult to do multimedia things. Ron says, "Nobody quite knew what to do with it or what it was. Bookshelf was just a godsend when it came out in 1987." Bookshelf contained a dictionary, a thesaurus, and a book of quotations, among other features. "It was perfect for CD-ROM. It was the only real application for CD-ROM. We had all been racking our brains out trying to figure out what applications we could do for CD-ROM that people could actually use. Everybody could use Bookshelf, especially people who did a lot of writing. Bookshelf was an application that gave people other ideas of what could be done with CD-ROM technology."

Microsoft Press, headed by Min Yee, wanted to develop products for CD-ROM as well as CD-I. So did Tom Lopez's CD-ROM group. Turf wars became inevitable. Ron explains, "There was some indecision as to who should be controlling the direction of CD-ROM technology. Tom Lopez had enormous contacts within the industry. He worked with them to develop the hardware and to make the CD-ROM drive more usable so that people would buy it. Every year, Min and Tom were responsible for Microsoft's CD-ROM conference. Tom always worked hard to have something that was spectacular—something he could announce and keep Microsoft in the limelight and at the forefront of CD-ROM technology. But Min, on the other hand, had the responsibility to develop new products, and some ideas for the CD-ROM technology— products that showed what could be done with CD-ROM. Min was developing a lot of products and was always in the forefront." Min Yee was responsible for licensing an encyclopedia for CD-ROM. He was also responsible for the content and look and feel of the products or applications. Even though Microsoft had created two groups, Press and the CD-ROM group, and had designated responsibilities for each group, infighting erupted. Ron observed the process. "Min was in charge of publishing, so he thought he should be in charge of it. Tom was the head of the CD-ROM group, and he thought he should be the one in charge. It was just like any other company in that regard—fighting went on for control."

With his knowledge of hardware and software, Ron understood the problems of each side. He also had knowledge of and experience with interactive videodiscs. He knew how to develop the CD-ROM technology. At Press, he worked on the encyclopedia project that would eventually become Encarta. It was a daunting task. Min Yee needed to find an encyclopedia to license. Ron remembers how difficult that was. "The encyclopedia companies were just scared to death to license their material to us. They were afraid of copying and piracy. Finally, Min Yee was able to license the content of *Funk and Wagnall's*."

When Ron set to work putting the text files onto CD-ROM, he ran into many problems. "All of the text was on typesetting pages," Ron notes. "If they made changes, they just stuck it on the end of the tape. There were all these typesetting codes. In order to input all this stuff we had to reorganize it and give it some structure. Some codes were undefined and nobody knew what the hell they were! You'd make a few calls to find out. Then you'd just write a program and crank it through."

Special characters presented another problem for Ron. When CD-ROM first came out, there were certain characters that could not be used because the drive would mistake them for a command. Files that had been generated to create books were not designed so that they could be converted to text files and put on a CD-ROM. Another problem was special characters such as those found in chemistry and physics. Ron notes, "It's not like a book. You had to be able to display them on a screen. Sometimes it drove me crazy." But Ron is persistent and organized, and he was able to prevail.

The biggest problem was pictures and sound. "Most people don't realize that encyclopedia companies do not own the pictures. They license most of them from a large distributor such as the Bettmann Archives. So *Funk & Wagnall's* had text, but no pictures. Sound cards were not yet perfected, so we were stuck with CD audio, which took up a great deal of space. Once we had pictures and sound, we had to figure out a way to use that picture or sound over again or we would run out of space. We figured it out." By 1993, Encarta had sold approximately 350,000 copies and generated about $25 million in revenue. The following year, the number of copies sold jumped to a million.

As technology progressed, the graphics capabilities and the speed of computers improved. Ron notes, "One thing typical of Microsoft was that we designed for the future rather than the present. It's an easy way out of dealing with a specific problem. You know the technology will get better, so why waste your time designing for a slow CD-ROM drive? Design for a CD-ROM drive that is six to twelve times faster; don't bang your head against the wall."

Everyone at Microsoft worked hard, including Ron. However, he worked only a 40-hour week. "My wife kids me about being naive," says Ron. "I simply didn't know that I was supposed to work longer than a forty-hour week. I didn't work nights or weekends." Ron was a little bit older than most of his peers. "When I was younger, I would work twenty-four hours a day. I didn't have a wife or children. It was natural to work that hard. At Microsoft I never felt the pressure to work longer hours, but if they needed me, I would. Right before I retired I was trying to set up a meeting with Mike Maples, who was the VP in charge of applications. He asked if we could get together on Saturday. 'Saturday?' I said. It really took me back," Ron says and laughs hard. "A person could work twenty-four hours a day for the rest of his life. There's always something to do. You have to decide when to stop and do something else. It will get done. The schedules that Microsoft had were always such a mess that you rarely met your schedule anyway. The schedules were too short and idealistic. A lot of young people at Microsoft liked to work long hours because they enjoyed the work so much and the facilities were conducive to that. I was in my forties and most people were in their twenties. I had a family and a life outside of Microsoft."

Ron was very happy working for Press. "You could not ask for a better boss than Min Yee," Ron says and smiles. "The guy is *wonderful.* He knows how to keep people happy and he knows how to get things done. He makes you feel like you're important. If you need anything, he'll do his best to get it for you. I was very comfortable at Press."

The environment at Press was far different than the environment at the rest of Microsoft. Microsoft was considered a programmer's company. Press was made up of literary types—writers and editors. In other divisions, some of the staff tended to look down their noses at Press. Ron explains, "There was a whole different mindset and intelligence at Press than that of the developers. The Press people had more artistic and aesthetic backgrounds and it was more of a social environment. I loved Press, but I didn't realize until I left how good it really was. We had parties and retreats. People seemed to care about the group. It was smaller and more relaxed. Of course, all that has changed now. It's a much larger group now and more profit-driven."

Ron disliked managing people. "I hated being a manager. I like being friends with people. But you can't be friends with people and be their manager too. You need to be aware of how you treat people—the smallest detail can have a big effect in the long run. It's unfortunate because it turns you into someone who is somewhat plastic— someone who doesn't have much depth and someone who doesn't want to get personally involved with people. Working within a large group teaches you to treat people delicately." Ron was a very hands-off manager. "I assumed that if I hired people, then they were capable. If they had any problems, I wanted them to let me know about them. I gave them a lot of freedom. In general, it worked out. But some people like more direction."

If Ron disliked managing people, he detested the six-month review system. He says caustically, "I thought it was this New Age, self-help sort of crap. It was a waste of time. I could never really get into it. I had never, ever worked for a company that had a review system. It was great if you got a 4.0. I never did well on my reviews because I never really put anything into them. I just rewrote my review from the previous year."

Ron was more of a technical person and wanted to work with a more technical group, even though he enjoyed his stint at Press. So Ron decided to go to work as a software developer in Tom Lopez's CD-ROM group, which had been formed in 1985. The CD-ROM group worked on designing tools to develop software, authoring systems, and the indexing of software. Ron worked on a multimedia project, the US West Yellow Pages. He says, "It was exploring new technology." People from US West came and scanned pictures and developed audio for the multimedia. "The project was sort of a precursor to the Internet. Users could search a screen for items in the Yellow Pages and be shown a list of companies that had those products or services."

Ron also worked on a database for US West called Omega, which was developed for Windows by Microsoft and was meant to compete with all the other database programs. "Omega was in its infancy and crashed a lot. I gave the bug reports, and I was working very hard to develop the piece of software. But Omega was difficult to use. We delivered the product to US West, but they never used it. I think they just chalked the project up to research," Ron says. This was typical of Ron's work at Microsoft. He was often used to explore new and emerging technology, both for hardware and software. It was understood that some products would become hits and others would not, but in order for Microsoft to maintain its leadership position in its field, it had to take risks. And Ron, with his twin areas of expertise, was perfectly suited to keep Microsoft on the cutting edge.

Soon after that, in 1989, Ron joined the Computer-Based Training Group as a developer. Ron helped develop software that would run tutorials and training sessions on the computer. The end user could learn to use Microsoft products such as Works and Word in an efficient way.

Ron was unhappy with the bureaucracy he found within the CBT group. "Our manager was good at delegating things for people to do, but she wasn't very good at delegating authority. She would have a lot of people working on different things, but she'd usually have to have the last word on something rather than let you die or stand on your own. When we went on business trips, we had to share rooms! I was a mature person; I'd never been required to do that at any other company. By 1988–89, bureaucracy just engulfed the CBT group," Ron notes.

While he was with the CBT group, Ron helped develop multimedia operating systems. They used them to create a multimedia tutorial for Works. Ron became the interface person between his group and the multimedia group. "I was a technical troubleshooter. I tried to let the multimedia group know what we needed from a technical standpoint. I helped the people in the CBT group understand what the software would do. I'd help them learn it and show them how to use it. It was hard. As part of Microsoft, we wanted to have special consideration. We wanted to be treated better than the others that the multimedia group was working with. We wanted to have more input into what the system was going to do," Ron says.

Ron also developed sound studios. While at CBT he hired someone to help him set up a sound stage. Together, they set up a small sound-recording studio where they did voices for the tutorial. "The tutorial had characters, or guides, that would take the user through the tutorial." Ron laughs and says, "We found people at Microsoft who had interesting voices. They'd come over and read and we'd record them."

Ron downplays his achievements at the company. He says, "I don't think I had any key achievements at

Microsoft. Because of the position I was in, I was always involved with new, emerging technology. I usually wasn't given mature technology to develop a product for. It was always, 'Here's this idea these people have. Is it any good, and do you think we can do anything with it?' I'd take a look at it and see what we could or could not do with it. I was a technical manager who was a resource for questions relating to the technology. I acted as an interface, as I understood both software and hardware."

Ron considers Microsoft one of the better companies in the industry to work for. "You get so many benefits at Microsoft," Ron says. "They have excellent health insurance, stock options, cafeterias, free beverages, and so on. People have their own offices and the best computers and printers to work with. The campus setting is a brilliant idea. People are loyal to their colleges, aren't they? I think people feel like it's a personal thing. They feel well taken care of by Microsoft. They have respect for the company."

But one thorny personnel issue was that of freelancers. Microsoft had always used freelancers in all divisions in the company. "It was a way for the company to save money because they had such a good benefit package for full-time employees," says Ron. However, about 1988, the IRS stepped in and told Microsoft that the practice was not legal. Ron explains, "It was legal to hire freelancers, but the IRS had a very narrow definition of what a freelancer was. To be a freelancer, you had to meet certain criteria. None of those people fit into that category." The IRS informed Microsoft that it had to hire these freelancers as permanent employees. "That caused some really serious problems for Microsoft for many months," says Ron. "If the freelancers left, that meant about half of the workforce would be leaving." Microsoft decided to place all of its freelancers with temporary agencies and then hire them through the agencies when needed.

"I think a lot of the bad feelings people have about Microsoft are due to ignorance of what the computer industry is like," Ron states. "To try to force Microsoft to be fairer in the marketplace is not possible. It's naive thinking. When a big company like Boeing buys software like Windows or Word or Excel, they won't put it out to bid each year like they would a table or a chair. They buy a piece of software and that's what they're going to stick with. They're not going to go from Word to WordPerfect and back again. They won't keep putting people through the learning curve. It takes a year to learn a new piece of software, if you're lucky. Switching software would drive employees crazy, and the company would lose a ton of money. Microsoft does play hardball, but they have to keep on top. Microsoft is the top dog, and envy goes with the territory."

But by 1990, Ron was burned out. "I was just tired of computers—I'd spent my whole life working with them. I was forty years old and it wasn't fun anymore. The mistake I made was getting into management and out of development. I think that caused me to get tired of it all."

Ron left Microsoft and its politics behind. But Ron understands why Microsoft employees work so hard. "I think they really believe in what they are doing. It's kind of an altruistic feeling. Apple employees were called, 'evangelists.' That was their title," Ron says. "Microsoft didn't carry it that far, but I think people have a very personal commitment to what they are doing. It was a generation of technical people who just loved what they were doing."

On balance, Ron enjoyed his Microsoft experience. "When I was first hired, I was thrilled. I always enjoyed the prestige and recognition I got from working at Microsoft."

Life after Microsoft

In retirement, Ron is happy to be able to live a simpler life devoted to family and hobbies, such as woodworking. He is sought after for his fine cabinetry work. Min Yee owns a replica of the Parthenon that Ron made as a bookshelf. Ron and his wife, Joy, live in a landmark home in Seattle and care for their mothers. They also enjoy spending time with their children. Ron travels frequently around the world to hike, and he especially enjoys the trails in Hawaii.

Because he was older than many when he joined Microsoft and therefore older when he retired, Ron relishes the quiet and the security that his wealth has brought him. He says, "My wife Joy and I came from families that struggled to make life better for their children. It would not be pleasant to give up the comforts we have, but, fortunately, everything is paid for!"

Paul Sribhibhadh

"The Diplomat"

———————————————◼———————————————

Microsoft 1987–1997

Product Manager, XENIX

Group Manager, OS/2 LAN Manager,
OS/2 Marketing for the Government Market

Business Development Manager,
Asia Pacific Region

General Manager, Thailand

Paul Sribhibhadh

"The Diplomat"

Paul Sribhibhadh grew up in Thailand and moved to the United States in his late teens. He is of average height, slim, and his graceful movements are enhanced by his extensive practice of the martial arts. He has an engaging sense of humor. Paul is Thai-Chinese and the son of a diplomat. His personal and business philosophies draw on both Eastern and Western thought.

Paul has worked for three giants in the high-tech industry: IBM, Intel, and Microsoft. His observations of the three companies are keen and insightful.

Paul helped to define and deliver Microsoft's desktop and minicomputer integration strategy. He successfully got UNIX technology incorporated into OS/2. This UNIX technology was the key to entering government markets around the world.

He brought LAN Manager to market.

As Microsoft's general manager of Thailand, Paul grew the business in Thailand from $100,000 to $20 million in five years.

After retiring in 1997, Paul and his family remained in

Thailand. His goal is to bring technology and education to his country. His heart has always been with the developing countries in Southeast Asia.

The Path to Microsoft

Paul Sribhibhadh's father worked for the Thai government. He served as a cabinet member overseeing the Ministry of Agriculture under Prime Minister Kriengsak Chomanan in the mid-1970s, and was a diplomat from Thailand with the United Nations in Rome, Italy. Paul grew up and completed high school in Thailand, and he emulates his father's love and respect for his country. When Paul moved to the United States in 1975, he attended the University of Washington in Seattle as a computer science major.

In 1979, a young man named Bill Gates came to speak to Paul's class at the University of Washington. He gave a talk on the future of computing. Paul says, "He talked about the revolution created by the microprocessor and he talked about BASIC. What he was saying was going right over our heads. We thought, 'He looks like he's our age and he's talking about some kind of computing revolution! What revolution? We already have the DEC VAX minicomputer here today.' He discussed using a microcomputer in PCs and that it was going to be the wave of the future. We thought, 'No way!' He'd written BASIC for the microcomputer, and we all thought that BASIC was a Mickey Mouse language. 'B' as in 'beginner'—we kind of snickered. Real programmers used Pascal or C." Paul stops to laugh at the memory. "But he was so excited and enthusiastic that it was kind of addicting. He was very animated. He had a lot of enthusiasm for things that the ordinary person could do. He could have become just as excited about mainframes, as there was still a lot to be done to them. We thought he was very deep!" The audience had been moved 180 degrees in the course of Gates's presentation.

After graduating from the University of Washington, Paul went to work for IBM as a software developer in San Jose, California, and Tucson, Arizona. He wrote software for the mainframe computers. He found the work atmosphere there very stifling. He says, "Technically, you couldn't suggest things. You could make suggestions to your boss who in turn would convey them on. The environment was too structured and hierarchical. There was a lot of protocol and etiquette to follow. It was kind of like the government. If I wrote something, I had to have it checked for the proper tone, the proper grammar, and make sure that it conveyed the right message to the right person and didn't make my boss look bad. It was very tough to get things done there." At the time, IBM had invested in Intel and picked up the 8088 chip to make the first IBM PC. "IBM could have gone to Motorola for the chip," recalls Paul. "It was the first break for Intel, as they were struggling. They needed money and along comes Big Blue." And then, in another historic decision, IBM went to Microsoft to get DOS.

While he was with IBM, Paul took a leave of absence and attended graduate school at Northwestern. He completed his graduate degree in one year. He was interested in sales and marketing and interviewed with Hewlett-Packard, Procter & Gamble, and Intel. He decided to work in information technology for Intel as a product marketing engineer. He had to know the technical side and become involved with product specifications as well. "I wanted to work in the rough-and-tumble environment at Intel. They have a culture called 'constructive confrontation,' which is Andy Grove's management style. You could confront each other, yell at each other, but at the end of the day, you were just going after the issues. I didn't want to work in a Mr. Nice Guy environment. I thought Intel would be more open and lead to more creativity."

Still, it took Paul a little while to get used to the aggressive kind of environment he found at Intel. "You could argue with anybody! The confrontation style was difficult for an Asian who was raised to be courteous, humble, and respect authority. The workplaces were all open, just cubicles. We only used closed offices when we had meetings. They wanted everything to be open and accessible. But we could do things very quickly there."

At Intel he worked on software development tools and local area networking (LAN) software and hardware, in which cards were put into a PC to allow it to be hooked up to other PCs. "Despite having LAN products, Intel was not committed to expanding its software side of the business at the time. They were interested in the chips and printed circuit boards. But a chip is just a chip unless you have people who want to use it."

Paul worked with Paul Maritz, who was in charge of research and development (R&D). "Maritz became disenchanted with the management at Intel because of the emphasis on hardware at the expense of software. He left to form a software start-up, but ended up working for Microsoft before his company got started. Most of us mistakenly thought that companies like Microsoft who made products for general consumers were not serious companies," Paul recalls, not knowing at the time he would follow in Maritz's footsteps.

While living in Hillsboro, Oregon, and working for Intel, Paul and his wife Filomena decided to look for jobs in the Seattle area. "Fil's a physician, and we felt there would be more career opportunities for her in Seattle," says Paul. In 1987, Paul began a series of interviews with Boeing

Computer Services. "I got a call from Microsoft. Paul Maritz put me in touch with some people. I was curious as to why Paul would join Microsoft. He simply told me that the guy he worked for—Steve Ballmer—was a super-smart guy. And I thought Paul was already a really smart guy. This I had to see for myself."

Paul agreed to interview at Microsoft. "I wasn't serious about Microsoft," Paul recalls. "I interviewed with some of the directors, and then I interviewed with Steve Ballmer. He challenged me on some of the software and other products at Intel. I don't know . . . maybe I got defensive. I told him he didn't know what he was talking about and that he didn't have the right information to base his opinions on. He just laughed at me and said, 'Oh! So you don't think I know what I'm talking about?' He was a really good sport about it and didn't get mad at me. Later, Paul Maritz asked me how my interview with Steve went. I said, 'I got into an argument with him, so I don't feel very hopeful about this job. But let's keep in touch.'" Paul chuckles. "I almost blew it the second time!" (He counts the first time as not attempting to join Microsoft right after graduating from the University of Washington in 1980.) "But to my amazement, they offered me the job. I asked Paul Maritz, why on earth, after that interview, would they do that? He said, 'Steve likes you!' I told my wife it was probably *fate* that I would go to work at Microsoft."

Life at Microsoft

In 1987, Paul was hired as the Worldwide product manager for XENIX. XENIX is Microsoft's version of the UNIX operating system it licensed from AT&T and implemented on computers using the X86 Intel microprocessor. UNIX was a popular multitasking, multiuser operating system that promised application portability across chip archi-tectures like Motorola's 68000, Sun's SPARC, and Silicon Graphic's MIPS chip families. Paul went to work for the Systems Division in Redmond and reported to his old friend from Intel, Paul Maritz, the director of XENIX. His first responsibility was to phase out XENIX 286. "We had to get rid of the 16-bit 80286 and go to the 32-bit 80386. The good news was that there was still some life left in the 80286, so we milked it. We built up a new 32-bit operat-ing system, XENIX 386—the first 32-bit operating system to come from Microsoft for the volume market. Bill Gates had this vision that Microsoft would create a standard advanced portable operating system for all of the micro-processor-based PC platforms."

Five months into his job at Microsoft, Paul was asked to attend a high-level meeting in France, scheduled during Microsoft's annual International Sales Meeting, where he was to give a talk on the direction of Microsoft's XENIX technology. "I was supposed to go on to Italy to visit Olivetti, our biggest European customer, as they were having second thoughts about whether to stay with us or use AT&T's generic UNIX operating system.

"In France, we had the meeting about how to approach them. I was there to present the strategy for XENIX. We really wanted to convince Olivetti to stay with us. Bill was at the meeting, but I had never met him to speak to before. I launched into my talk, and by my fourth sen-tence, Bill just started *reaming* me! I thought, 'My career is over!' *I didn't even know what I had done wrong.* While Bill was yelling at me, I couldn't say anything. I looked over at Jeremy Butler, the senior VP for International, because he and I had discussed the issues before we left Redmond. He just looked the other way! I looked at Bernard Vergnes, the director for France. He just looked down!" Paul stops to laugh at the unsettling memory. "I thought, 'The end! Everybody's abandoned me!' Then, after about ten minutes, Bill stopped. He said, 'Tell me again what the problem is.' I took a deep breath and went through the same process. I could see Bill was trying not to explode again. Finally he said, 'Hmmm. I guess that is a problem.' "

Bill realized that Olivetti was concerned about the compatibility of Microsoft's XENIX for the range of their products. XENIX ran only on the PC platforms, whereas Olivetti was using AT&T's version, UNIX, on their larger machines. Olivetti was trying to decide whether to just make it easy and use AT&T's version on all of their platforms.

Paul recalls, "Blood came back into my face. It actually turned out to be a very productive session. Bill began brainstorming and he was really brilliant. If Olivetti was not sure how serious we were about our XENIX operating systems business, they would go with AT&T. Bill showed that we looked at *all* the issues. I learned that he will first challenge you and expect you to stand up and be able to defend your position. I saw that the problems we were having were much bigger than I could handle by myself. We got a grip on it and finally told Olivetti that we were serious about our operating systems business and managed to convince them to stay with XENIX. Olivetti was convinced that if Microsoft were committed to XENIX, we would be able to create a marketwide standard for the multiuser, just as we did with MS-DOS for the PC market."

Another development in the XENIX business was the Santa Cruz Operation (SCO), a company in California that had the exclusive right to sell XENIX operating systems and business applications into the retail channel for Microsoft. Paul says, "Microsoft likes to take software and license it to another person with a private label on it called the OEM. It would be packaged by the company and then go through their distribution channel. Microsoft did not have to invest in building up a team to go after the distribution channel." It was Paul's brainchild to sell to SCO, but keep shares in the company, get a position on the board of directors, and pick up royalty checks.

In 1989, Paul joined the networking group as group manager for OS/2 LAN (local area network). The LAN market was exploding with the advances in the PC technology and the need for organizations to interconnect their PCs. It was a very new business for Microsoft. However, Microsoft knew it had to become a major player in this segment because it would be critical for organizational customers in the near future. Paul says, "I don't think we knew where we wanted to go with the networking business. We just jumped in because it was a very fast growing area. We didn't quite understand what it was about. The idea was, 'We've got some smart cooks in the kitchen and they'll figure out what to make.' "

At the time, Novell Inc.'s NetWare was king of the LAN operating system. Novell focused only on the software business and was growing in excess of 200 percent per year. Paul recalls, "With OS/2, Microsoft thought they had a really good operating system, better than MS-DOS. LAN Manager was the name of the networking product that ran on top of OS/2. We were trying to compete with Novell, but it was very, very tough. Bill Gates also figured that if we let Novell conquer the server operating system, it might shut off the chances for OS/2 in that market. Novell was selling more effectively through the well-established network called value-added resellers. We tried to rush the software out too fast. There was a real sense of urgency. Looking back on our early attempts to compete in the LAN OS market, I think the marketing actually preceded the product. The product was not quite ready with the features and speed to match Novell's Net-

Ware, although we promoted it very heavily. We learned that the old-channel strategy for LAN—selling through OEMs—didn't work and that quality does count. We hardly made an impact in the market early on. Everybody had some pretty nasty scars from that." Despite the misguided foray against Novell, Paul continued to market LAN Manager and OS/2. Internationally, he worked with Ida Cole, VP of Marketing, to launch and market the product, which did become successful.

In the United States, Paul's responsibility was to convince the U.S. government to consider using OS/2. The U.S. government was very much a UNIX market. Paul frequently flew to Washington, D.C., and held high-level meetings with government officials and representatives from the military. He convinced Steve Ballmer and Bill Gates to accompany him. "It took a while to convince the government," says Paul. "You can't convince someone by just telling them once, especially if they are biased against your products. Our strategy was to blanket them, to talk with them repeatedly. Bill and Steve would explain things, answer questions, and create what I called 'echo chambers.' If you echo something in a closed room enough times, people begin to incorporate that in their thinking. Pretty soon, you can see rear admirals starting to echo. They mix our ideas in with theirs and all of a sudden, it's their idea. It worked!"

The U.S. government believed in having open standards, which meant that its computers could run on multiple platforms such as computers from Sun, IBM, HP, Digital, and Silicon Graphics. Applications products such as word processors could be developed to run, for example, on IBM's UNIX and ported or moved over to hardware from, say, Hewlett-Packard, which also ran UNIX. This in effect allows you to write an application once and run it on multiple vendors' machines. Paul explains the government's hesitation about Microsoft. "The government saw OS/2 as a closed, proprietary technology that only belonged to Microsoft and IBM. It wasn't open. They had established the Federal Information Processing Standards, or FIPS, which were the government computing standards that every agency had to comply with in any procurement of IT systems. Unfortunately for MS, FIPS was mostly based on POSIX (derived from UNIX), which meant that OS/2 would be excluded if we didn't do something about POSIX. My task was to go there and make sure they didn't close the door on OS/2. It was going to be the next strategic operating system for Microsoft. But Microsoft was just too identified with MS-DOS for desktops. The government wanted to have UNIX for bigger machines. They thought MS-DOS was something they had to accept as a de facto standard for PCs, but they didn't have to accept OS/2. Even though Microsoft was successful then, it wasn't as powerful as IBM or Digital or the UNIX system. Consequently, besides the constant visits by our executives and countless meetings to persuade the powers to be in government, we also created a strategy to add the POSIX standard into OS/2. This was implemented in OS/2 version 2.1—and subsequently incorporated into Windows NT—and this version of OS/2 was sold to the government."

Paul continues, "But it was a bumpy road to success in the government sector. One leading IT publication for the government sector, *Government Computer News* (*GCN*), was constantly publishing stories critical of OS/2. To change this, Marty Taucher, a Microsoft spokesperson, and I arranged a meeting with the chief editor. He proceeded to tell Bill Gates why the government should stick with UNIX and the open standard policy. Paul remembers the meeting well. "When he finished speaking, the editor turned to Bill and said, 'What do you think, Bill?' Bill didn't say a *word*. He just steepled his fingers and rocked back and forth in his chair. Finally, very deliberately and slowly he said, 'That's the stupidest thing I've ever heard.' Paul stops to laugh. "We almost fell off our seats. There were sirens going off in our heads, 'Damage control! Damage control!' We had to shut down the conversation. I think the editor was trying too hard to impress Bill, as he'd never met him before. Needless to say, we had to do a lot of 'massaging' after that!" It all worked out. The government decided it was open to buying OS/2 in all IT procurements.

Another key achievement for Paul and his group was getting the second-generation networking products (OS/2 LAN Manager v2.0 and TCP/IP) out into the world. "We got Compaq, the leading network server computer vendor, to sign on, so our key event was launching a worldwide product with them. Actually, they thought it was their idea. When you have that kind of key product, there are many, many people who are involved. Steve and Bill got involved. It's really a group effort and achievement."

Paul worked hard at Microsoft. "I worked twelve-hour days unless we were developing a product or getting ready to launch a product, and then we'd work sixteen hours a day. We lived there. We lived on Coke, coffee, and pizza—in my case, we added fried rice and Thai noodles. We were a very international group, with British, Canadian, Chinese, German, and Swedish developers working with us. We'd play cricket and bowling in the hallways. We had to do something to keep from going crazy. No matter how tough it got, we always delivered. Those are very fond memories."

When Paul first started working, his goal was to get 10 years of work experience and then help the developing countries in Southeast Asia with emerging technologies. He says, "I cared about that region more than the average person at Microsoft, since I grew up there. My heart was really with the developing countries, especially Southeast Asia." In 1991, Paul talked with Rick Tsang, the regional manager of Asia Pacific. "Rick was thinking about expanding and asking for more resources in Asia Pacific. Microsoft didn't seem very serious about Southeast Asia at that time. Everything was sort of lumped together into a very small business."

Paul took the job of business development manager and began traveling frequently to Southeast Asia. "It was grueling, but also a lot of fun. I traveled every month. It's tough to talk about how Microsoft management viewed Southeast Asia, though. We got the feeling that the people brought in to look after Asia were not really committed to understanding the nuances of the markets or how the customers behaved. A lot of people just wanted to slam numbers. They didn't want to waste a lot of time with people and building relationships. It's a Western approach. It was a short-term approach rather than a long-term approach."

Paul and others working in Asia constantly confronted the issues of piracy—as high as 95 percent in all countries except for Singapore—and corruption. He struggled with how these factors affected working relationships. "Pretty soon, a lot of our managers just thought everybody out there was bad. They'd start talking to customers and associates with that kind of attitude. When you do that to people in an Asian culture, they'll politely close the door. Their way of doing business is different. I used to wonder why Microsoft hired certain individuals to run those regions. They really needed to understand the markets in much more meaningful ways."

Paul understood that his career at Microsoft took a toll on his family. "There's a lot of sacrifice from the family side. If I didn't have a really understanding wife, it would have been the end of our marriage. One time she asked me if I was enjoying my job. She said, 'Sometimes you're not a very nice person.'"

By 1993, Paul was ready to live in Asia again. He and his wife decided to move to Thailand, where Paul became the general manager of Microsoft Thailand. It was a dream come true for Paul to help his country. "It was time to move there. It was very difficult to do things from afar. Once you develop a market, you have to have local presence. You have to have local decisions being made and they need to be made quickly. I wrote a proposal for opening up an office in Thailand."

Paul single-handedly developed and implemented a business development model and convinced Microsoft senior management to invest in Thailand. He developed a Microsoft Thai-language product plan and convinced senior management to fund the implementation of his plans. He built a Microsoft subsidiary in Thailand, trained and developed local employees, and was officially recognized by the Thai government for his business contribution to the country. "When you're out there in the field, it's guerrilla marketing at its best—it's just pure adrenaline. You are on the front line. You're traveling around trying to develop a business. Those were the pioneering days. A lot of people didn't know about Microsoft. There was no infrastructure. You had to be extremely resourceful. Teamwork was crucial."

Paul wanted to get involved in Thai policymaking at the national level and perhaps even enter politics. "I proved myself at Microsoft. If you're not good at Microsoft, you're out. I always felt I'd be more effective in the developing countries than in the developed countries. The Western business philosophy and Bill's vision provide people with the satisfaction of an accomplished task. The Eastern philosophy says you have to have wholeness as well. You don't get that at Microsoft. While I was in International, I felt like I was on some kind of combat mission instead of just trying to come up with the best product." But Paul grew the business from $1 million to about $30 million in three and a half years, in a market rife with software piracy, low consumption, and complex product requirements.

As the general manager of Thailand, Paul put into action his unique synthesis of Eastern and Western business philosophies. "I always tried to keep the human element in business. You have to make sure, in Asia especially, that you give the other person respect. Even if you're telling them you have to bust them—it's all in your approach. I spent a lot of time on delivery. Asians don't like a confrontational approach. I also tried to help the other person first. I didn't go in there and ask for something right away. It wasn't, 'This is what *I* want.' *No! No! No!* It's, 'What do *you* want?' I learned that if you give first, they'll bend over backwards to help you. I'd win their trust. But when I managed people I also wanted camaraderie, but not total convergence of thought. To me, that's being brain dead. People appreciate it if you worry about their development. My job was to develop them as a manager and to help them promote themselves.

"I never thought my life would turn out like this. I'm forty-one years old and I have enough energy left to help the developing countries in IT and education. The Asian work ethic is to simply work hard and see what happens. I've learned so much from my experiences with IBM, Intel, and especially Microsoft. I never thought I'd be financially independent at such a young age. I worked hard and accumulated wealth, so now it's time to make a contribution to society. I have been very, very lucky."

Life after Microsoft

Paul started two software companies in Thailand, one for education and one for business development. He has also invested venture capital in a few Internet start-ups in the United States. There are 65 million people in Thailand, and only 3 million PCs have been sold. "It's an infant industry in Thailand," Paul notes. "I'm thinking about how I can empower people so they can learn things and help themselves. Our king is beloved and benevolent, but he won't live forever. The old-style bureaucrats and corrupt politicians still run things. We need a new breed of people who will push for change and create a fairer distribution of education and wealth." Being able to help his country is a dream come true for Paul.

Paul has also spearheaded the development of a national computer software association (the Association of Thai Software Industry) based in Bangkok.

And, not least, after his demanding years at Microsoft, Paul enjoys getting back to sports and spending ample time with his wife Fil, their two daughters, his parents, and his extended family.

RUSSELL STEELE

"The Musician"

Microsoft: 1986–1994

Publishing Systems Manager

Production Manager, Microsoft Press
International

RUSSELL STEELE

"The Musician"

Russell Steele wears his hair tied in a ponytail, dresses in jeans, and sports an earring. When he was younger, he was a rock musician playing rhythm guitar in bands that had a wide range of musical styles. He is friendly, honest, and wise beyond his 36 years. He has worked full time since he was a sophomore in high school.

Russell does not have a college degree, a rare thing at Microsoft. When he became production manager at Microsoft Press, Russell was very young and enthusiastic about newly emerging technologies. Over time, he became frustrated with those at Press who were intimidated by the new technologies and resisted change.

Today, Russell owns and operates his own helicopter company. He uses a hands-on approach to teach his students the often dangerous skill of flying a helicopter. He also hopes to resume his passion as a guitarist and head of a rock band.

The Path to Microsoft

Russell Steele grew up in Roseburg, Oregon. He good-naturedly refers to his background as "upper lower class." Russell credits his parents for his success. "They never told me I couldn't do anything. Not in a spoiled sort of way, but just believing in me. They never told me I had to go to college to be a success." Russell's father is an ex-Marine and a diesel mechanic. His mother did the accounting for a local hospital.

In 1978, in junior high, Russell took a typing class and broke all records at the school by typing 102 words a minute on a manual typewriter. In his sophomore year, the journalism class needed someone to type all the articles for the school newspaper. "I begged the journalism teacher to allow me into his class even though you weren't supposed to until you were a junior. I showed him how quickly I could type, and they trained me on the typesetting equipment. I loved it so much that when I turned sixteen, I pleaded with the production manager of the daily newspaper, *The News-Review,* to give me a job."

While in high school, Russell worked full time at the newspaper. He used minicomputers, worked on production, and did manual layout design. Later, he became the editor for the weekly arts and entertainment tabloid.

After graduating from high school, Russell and his rock and roll band, called The Dangerous Penguins, moved to Eugene, Oregon. "We wanted to get noticed, and we were convinced the only way was to go to a worthy college town like Eugene. We all moved there—girlfriends and wives, too. I was married at the time." In Eugene, Russell did typesetting jobs to earn money. He founded a classified paper, *The Adventure Classifieds.* "Every time I'd pick up one of the local advertising papers I'd get so frustrated. Nothing was categorized. It was just thrown together. I started a little weekly advertising paper with categories such as "Fuel and Wood." I called my competitions' advertisers and asked them if they wanted to place ads for free for two weeks in my paper. I used a Kaypro [an early PC device] to compile the list of ads."

In 1984, the University of Oregon hired Russell as the production manager for the college newspaper, *The Daily Emerald.* It was a wholly owned, private corporation. The production department employed students, and for Russell's class they had the option of receiving either credits or a paycheck. Russell recalls, "I was twenty-one then, and one of the students got a great deal on a Mac 128K, which was in a huge box. It was supposed to be portable. It had no hard drive. I remember being dumbfounded that you could drag this thing called a 'mouse' and the screen would respond. Even then, I was chomping at the bit because I wanted it to go faster. I realized how limited its capacity was." With each position he took, Russell gained hands-on experience with the variety of computers available at the time.

In 1985, Russell's band dissolved. He and his wife wanted to move to San Francisco. Russell says, "I began responding to various publishing-related jobs in the *San Francisco Chronicle.* One was for a company called Micro–soft in Redmond, Washington. I didn't have a clue as to where Redmond was or what Microsoft was. Microsoft Press was a two-year-old start-up, and they were looking for a composition supervisor. I'd had experience with CCI [Computer Composition International] typesetting equipment, and that's what they were looking for. I applied, but I said to my wife, 'Don't worry, honey. I really do want to move to San Francisco. These guys will never respond.' "

A month later, after two telephone interviews, Microsoft asked Russell to come to Redmond for a series of in-person interviews. Russell remembers thinking, "Wow!

Cool! This company is so big they're going to fly me up, give me a hotel and a rental car. I was twenty-three years old, and I didn't know much about the mind-set beyond Eugene. I was really caught off guard that people could spend so much money just trying to find a recruit."

During his interviews at Microsoft, Russell felt very uncomfortable. "I actually had to borrow a suit and did the old take-out-the-earring thing and got a crew cut." Russell pauses to laugh at the memory. "I showed up with this dorky briefcase, and about the only thing I had in it was a copy of the morning newspaper and a few more resumes in case I had to hand one to someone. It wasn't like I actively used a briefcase in Eugene."

Russell was also uncomfortable with the interview questions. "It was this psychoanalytical bullshit. I'd never been exposed to that. I wasn't ready for things like, 'So tell me Russell, would you be willing to tell a white lie if it meant that you were going to be able to accomplish certain things? Would you tell white lies to your employees to be able to accomplish certain goals?' I was sitting there squirming and thinking, 'Are they looking for a particular answer?' " They told Russell they'd contact him within a week, but several weeks went by and Russell heard nothing from them. "I thought they didn't like me and that's why they weren't calling me back." But a few weeks later, Russell got a call from Human Resources at Microsoft and received a job offer. Russell says, "I told them I was interested but I didn't know what they had in mind salarywise. I really didn't know what to expect. It ended up being twice as much as I was making, which wasn't much. But I didn't realize the cost of living in the Seattle area was two to three times as much as in Eugene. You were paid less by Microsoft than if you took a similar job somewhere else. They supplemented your income with these pieces of candy called stock options."

Life at Microsoft

"Very quickly I had to settle in to being just me. You find out right away that there's no better place than Microsoft when it comes to having the freedom to be who you are. That's the thing that Microsoft has hands-down over the rest of the business world." Russell was employee number 1,047. "You could have an impact then. The company was still small enough that if your phone rang and you didn't answer it, they had a paging system in place."

For the first few years, Russell bought into the whole Microsoft culture. "I worked sixty to seventy hours a week," he says. "I was young and naive enough to do it. It cost me some things in my life. Working Saturdays and Sundays was not uncommon. For the first six months, my head was spinning with new information. And I was trying to fit inside a corporation. I was also taking on things that I had limited experience with or that I had not been in charge of before. I was acquainted with daily stress because of my background in newspapers. Every day there's a deadline. That's a benefit because you get to put it to rest. It's over with. At Microsoft, there's *never, never* an end to it. I remember thinking, 'If I could just get rid of these stacks on my desk, my life would be so much easier.' It never happens. It only continues to grow. You show your excellence and what do you get? You get more responsibility! At Microsoft, it's not written anywhere that you have to work that hard, but people do."

At Microsoft Press, Russell worked for Chris Banks, the senior director. Russell's first job was composition supervisor. Within six months he was promoted to publishing systems manager. Russell worked on the publishing production process, readying the text and graphics of the books for printing. When a manuscript was delivered in electronic format, Russell's group oversaw the edits, the artwork creation and incorporation, pagination, and delivery to the printing company. "In the early days," Russell says, "We delivered conventional linotronic output to the printing company." One of Russell's key achievements at Press was overseeing the transition to electronic prepress (EPP), which was the ability to deliver the book's paged files to the printing company on diskette. "The closer you remain to the original output during the printing process, the better off you'll be. We wanted to eliminate as many steps as possible." Russell and his team came up with a procedure to deliver on diskette with a plain-paper proof accompanying it to the printer for reference. "Back then, it was an extraordinary achievement," says Russell. In 1990, making books hadn't changed that much since Gutenberg.

When Russell first began working at Press, he found Min Yee, the publisher, working on a Macintosh. "He had a spreadsheet on the Mac, and I said, 'What could you possibly do with a Macintosh, play games?' He looked at me like, 'You little smart-ass!' Then he told me what they did with Macs in those days. I had lost sight of Macs because they were so expensive."

Russell began his day checking e-mails and voice mails. "You had no choice," he says. "You had to determine who was working until 9 P.M. the previous evening and had a problem only you could solve." Then he'd check on his schedule for the day. "I spent sixty to sixty-five percent of my time in meetings. Press was publishing sixty books a year. That was more than one book a week." Of the 60 titles, nearly one-third were new editions of previously released titles, such as Charles Petzold's *Programming Windows* or Van Wolverton's *Running MS-DOS*. Books ran the gamut in size from 250 to 900 pages in length.

Press dealt with code-based publishing and took a long, hard look at desktop publishing capabilities. "Since there were designers and electronic artists working in my group, I got to know about Macs, but I didn't really like Macs. I wanted to have some nice convertible platforms and run Windows on the machines. But there was no denying that the designers needed to use Macs because it was the best way to go at the time. Whenever Min Yee had problems with his Macs, especially with the font capabilities, I was the person sent in to solve the problems for him. The CD-ROM group was fairly new, and Ron Harding and Ed Kelly were getting ready for Bookshelf to come out. They were toying with scanning and such being incorporated into electronic media. They weren't sure what they were going to do with it at the time, but Min wanted to show how this information could be output on an electronic device of some sort. We were trying to show the bridges that existed so Min could continue to make the argument as to why the CD-ROM group should be kept. Min really went through it with CD-ROM.

"It's the people in your group who make you who you are," observes Russell. "One of the most wonderful people in my life is a gal named Jean Trenary. I hired her within four months of coming to Microsoft. In all my years of managing, before and during Microsoft, I had over a hundred employees who had to answer to me, and Jean was, hands down, the most important person I ever worked with. She came in as a composition supervisor when I was promoted to publishing systems manager. I also worked with some wonderful freelance contractors who would give an arm and a leg for you. Some eventually became employees as openings occurred. Chris Banks [former senior director] and I are still good friends. Min Yee [former publisher] is just so incredibly present. I just love those guys."

Russell is proud of the work he did at Press. He particularly remembers working on the second edition of *Pro-*

gramming Windows. He worked with a brilliant person named Jeff Hinsch, who had developed a utility for capturing screen images so they could be converted into a graphic image and be embedded in the electronic text pages. "It was unlike anything other computer book publishers were doing at the time. These things are called 'screen dumps.' They're what you see in a computer book when you're reading along and the text says, 'Now, point your mouse at the right-hand corner of your screen . . . double click . . . and this is what you'll see.' Boom! They put the picture of that in your book. Jeff worked night and day on this. It was something that no one had ever done before with the publishing software we were using at the time, Magna, which was a PC-based version of CCI. Jeff and I and others worked long and hard to be able to incorporate these types of things and took great pride in being able to make books with these screen dumps. They were setting the industry standard for every other publisher who attempted to follow."

Another project that captivated Russell's enthusiasm was a project with Russell Borland, who was the in-house author for Press. Russell Steele says, "He went to the marketing department and told them he had an idea for a book and that they had a short window of opportunity. Russell had not only written a book about Microsoft Word, but he had also laid out the book, as he was a user of Word. He'd come up with the design. The screen dumps were in place. It was ready to go. It was a great opportunity, but there was a ton of resistance from people who did not want to work in the electronic world. Basically, Russell was challenging the marketing and editorial departments to work with electronic tools. But they continued to insist on a paper trail for their edits and plans. Russell and I pushed for the book to be assigned to a skunk works team who would step up to the challenge of editing the book on-line, on the fly, what I referred to in meetings as 'taking the ultimate responsibility.' Instead of being assigned to a team that could turn the title on a dime, the book took a more standard route and went to the printer four to six weeks later than we could have sent it. I'm sure we missed a serious chunk of sales because of the slower approach. It always came down to an argument about quality." Steele preached about the need for Press to define "quality." He believed that the sales opportunity for software books was very short, observing, "Your book needs to be on the shelf as soon as the software hits the shelf. Even if that means having a few mistakes, you still would have bigger sales. Fix some of the mistakes at reprint. You can't make bug-free software, so why strive for that in the book about the software? Needless to say, it wasn't a very popular theory."

By 1996, Press was doing on-line editing through all of the phases. Prior to that, certain people would not budge because they claimed there would be no editing trail. Russell had an answer for that. "Let's make one person ultimately responsible for this project and whatever edits they make to the file will stick." But Russell became increasingly frustrated. Responsibility at Press was spread so thin and across so may departments that there was no ultimate responsibility. "It was very easy to point fingers," says Russell.

Russell was dealing with issues of change and control. Historically, editors did not use computers. "A writer, a proofreader, and an editor know how to write, spell, and construct. You can't necessarily teach a computer to do all of those things. It was hard for them to see the need to change," Says Russell. But technology had changed all that.

Some of Russell's most exciting times at Press were teaching people how to do things or overseeing a transition phase. You have to develop things—you can't buy them off the shelf," says Russell. "When we first started doing plain-paper proofing at Press, not everything went smoothly. The page description language known as Post-Script was in its infancy on the Apple LaserWriter printers. We were using output from them as a bastard representation of what the final output was going to look like once we sent it to our linotronic imaging devices." But the laser printers could not emulate all the typefaces on the linotronic machines and would substitute certain symbols and Greek characters in place of things like curly quotes, mathematical symbols, and such. "This transitional phase was the perfect opportunity to win over the proof department," Russell recalls. "They needed to believe us when we told them that what they were marking as incorrect on the plain paper would actually become the expected characters once we created the final output on the Linotronic machines. This was when we made the transition to electronic incorporation of Mac-generated line art into PC-based text files, and my departments had a chance to shine in their coordination, communication, and interactions with other groups.

"I loved my job then because I was running three departments and there were fascinating technological changes taking place. All these things were keeping us on the leading edge of technology. I was completely jazzed by all that stuff."

While at Press, Russell continued to play in bands. "It was nice to have that artistic release," he says. During his last year at Microsoft, Russell trained to get his private helicopter license. "I realized that I had been working full time since I was sixteen. I had other jobs before I came to Microsoft. There are many, many people at Microsoft who had never worked anywhere else. They don't have any idea that what goes on at Microsoft is not 'normal.' It's not the real world." Russell pauses for a moment and continues. "There is no other place in the world where the expectations are as high and demanding as they are there. But there isn't an employee handbook that says you have to give a hundred and thirty percent. I began to see that I needed to make other things important in my life, not just my job. You're with your coworkers more than you are with your husband or wife."

Russell says with a smile, "But I wouldn't trade my experience at Microsoft for anything. When I decided to leave, I remember I just craved to take what I had experienced in that environment and go back into the daily newspaper business. The kind of rapid-fire decision making we used at Microsoft could be applied to a different industry. But somehow I've known since I was fourteen that there were things I wanted to be: a rock star, a publishing magnate, and a helicopter pilot. I've come close to fulfilling all three.

"If Bill was assassinated tomorrow, and that's what it would be, an assassination, people are going to dump their stock. They don't realize that Bill doesn't make every decision. It's a damn fine company, and they'd still turn out good products because Bill has surrounded himself with brilliant people. That's what makes the difference between a person being good or great. It's okay to have a vision, but if Bill didn't have people to help him carry out and communicate that vision, there would be no Microsoft."

Russell continues, "Microsoft likes to be the first to do something. At Press, we were one of the first ones to buy a fully digital camera and build a shooting studio for a book. That's what it's all about. Where Microsoft goes wrong is that it wanted to be the biggest and the best at everything. They have the money and the power to follow any whim. That rubs me wrong because of my upbringing. But then again, where is all my investment money? In Microsoft. I'm the worst all-eggs-in-one-basket investor you've ever seen. But you know what? Tell me I've done it *wrong*."

Life after Microsoft

Russell Steele owns and operates his own helicopter company, Cowboy Copters, located south of Boeing field in Seattle. Students spend approximately $8,500 to have Russell's company give them hands-on instruction in order to get a helicopter's license. When students make errors, it can be very dangerous for Russell, and he's had some near misses. What keeps him interested? "It's like flying in your dreams—you can hover, fly backwards, go straight vertical, or just fly around. You fly about five hundred feet off the ground, so what you see is much more intimate." The company supplements its income by piloting flights for aerial photographers.

Russell takes pride in looking after his friends who are between jobs or in need of help. He also gives to charitable organizations. "Bill Gates and Paul Allen can write checks for millions of dollars and have a wing of a library or hospital named after them. If you're worth billions of dollars, then giving away $10 million isn't that much. But if you've got a lot less and can give a friend a meal or a ride or some money, that's important. You never know when you might need them to help you."

Russell also intends to keep playing the guitar. "I still want to make a living crawling onto a stage each night with a guitar strapped around my neck. Someday I will." Considering Russell's history of determination and success, it's quite likely that he will do just that.

12

TRISH MILLINES DZIKO

"The Athlete"

■

Microsoft: 1988–1996

Software Tester

Program Manager

Content Manager, Technet

Senior Diversity Administrator

TRISH MILLINES DZIKO

"The Athlete"

Trish Millines Dziko is attractive, friendly, and forth-right. She is 41 years old, a former athlete who keeps herself in top physical condition and exudes health and vitality. She dresses simply, but with style. As a woman of color, she has experienced prejudice in the workplace and now devotes her time to helping people of color, especially children, advance in the world of technology. Trish is very action-oriented.

Trish began her career at Microsoft as a consultant in software testing and was later hired as a full-time employee. She has been a program manager for API Visual BASIC for SQL Server and for children's hardware tools such as Easy Ball. She was content manager for Technet and senior diversity administrator.

Trish left Microsoft to push for change in industry practices in hiring minorities. She and her partner, Jill Hull Dziko, started Technology Access Foundation (TAF), which gives children of color access to computer skills and has internship programs for teens. It is a dream come true for

Trish to help African Americans and other people of color find their place in the technology revolution.

The Path to Microsoft

Trish Millines grew up in the small seaside town of Belmar, New Jersey, whose main source of income is summer tourism. As with many small towns, people knew each other and were helpful and supportive. While Trish was in high school, her mother became ill. Members of the church and people from the community lent a helping hand. Trish says, "It was really hard because she got sick when I was sixteen years old. She couldn't work. I was trying to be a teenager, a basketball player, and go to college. I had to be the other adult in the house. I grew up without a father and was an only child."

When Trish was 17, her mother died. In spite of her situation, Trish always knew she was going to go to college and have a career. "That came from my mom. She was always pushing me to get an education so I didn't have to clean floors like she did. In my generation and family, our grandparents and parents really never had a chance at education. My Uncle Johnny was the only one who had graduated from college. When my mom died, there was no question that I'd continue with my education. That's what I was supposed to do."

After graduating from high school, Trish accepted a basketball scholarship to Monmouth University, the same school from which her uncle had graduated. Trish smiles and says, "It was a big deal. I had a great time there. My life revolved around basketball and studying." Trish started out as an electrical engineering major, but changed to computer sciences when she realized the EE labs were held at the same time as her basketball practice. "I chose the next best major," she says.

Trish's basketball coach looked after her and the other players. "She set up work-study for those of us who had no money. She made sure we went to our classes and kept up our grades." Trish's coach had refereed her high school basketball games and was one of the reasons she chose to go to Monmouth. "Right after my mom died, I knew somehow that I needed to stay close to home and be around people who cared for me."

When Trish graduated from Monmouth she wanted to join the Air Force. "My whole desire was to play basketball and fix airplanes." But her basketball coach talked her out of a career in the Air Force. "She said, 'You've been taken care of your whole life. It's time for you to go out there and stretch your wings.' She knew I was ready."

In 1979, heeding her coach's advice, Trish and a friend moved to Philadelphia, where Trish took a job as a programmer for Computer Science Corporation, a military contractor. Trish pauses as she remembers her first job experience. "I was prepared very well for programming, but I was not prepared for the real world of corporate America. I wasn't prepared for the sexism, racism, and the games you had to play to move up in a company. I had a friend, Mary, who was white. Her degree was in English, and the company taught her to program. She was making $10,000 a year more than I was! I was twenty-two years old. I didn't know what to do. I learned that if more than three African Americans got together, people would become suspicious. That really irritated me. I learned to talk just one-on-one with people. And if I hung out with my white friends, my black colleagues thought I was selling out. I was used to that, though, because I'd always had a mix of friends."

After six months, the company wanted Trish to spend half a year on a research boat in the Pacific testing a four-faced radar system. "That didn't appeal to me," she says. So Trish resigned.

While reading *Computer World* magazine, Trish found an application form for Hughes Aircraft Company in Tucson, Arizona, and filled it out. Two weeks later she received a telegram asking her to come for an interview. She was hired as a programmer and wrote software to test the Phoenix and the Tow missiles. She stayed there from 1980 to 1982. "Unfortunately I had a boss who was overtly racist," Trish says. "*It was the worst experience I had ever had.* He'd whisper things behind my back." Trish's face clouds over as she recalls the experience. "I was still just a year out of school and didn't really know how to handle it. I was fortunate to have coworkers there who kept the experience from being totally depressing." Trish declines to repeat her boss's racist comments.

Eventually, Trish ended up in the database group. "My boss there was great. She taught me how to get along in a corporation. It was the first time I used C computer language, which was very hot at the time. That's when I really learned how to take control of the computer.

"In 1982, I probably made the dumbest mistake of my life. I moved to San Francisco without a job during an economic recession. I sold my house in Tucson, bought a motor home, packed up the dogs and cat and moved." Trish shakes her head as she recalls her folly. She had a job offer, but felt the pay was too low to live in San Francisco. "I just took my chances to find a job." But it would take her eight months to find a job, and her resources were running low. "I'd park my motor home wherever I could. I was always getting ticketed. I ended up parking at the Marina with other people who were living in their cars. They taught me how to stretch food. We'd go to

Happy Hour at bars, buy a Coke, and get free food. I didn't have an address or a phone, so employers couldn't contact me. Finally, a headhunter helped me out. She was my office."

Trish took a job teaching Assembly computer language and was fired for not giving a few of her students A's. She felt they didn't deserve the grade. "That was pretty depressing. That was the first time I'd ever been fired." By that time, Trish had a studio apartment in Nob Hill and had managed to save some money. She then took a job as a software tester for Fortune Systems and says, "That was the single most important move that I made in my career. It introduced me to the PC industry." Trish learned the UNIX operating system and tested software there.

In 1984, the company went under. "At the time, there were a lot of successful computer start-ups that went under. The owners bought too many Ferraris or did too much cocaine." Trish decided it was time to leave San Francisco.

That year Trish visited a friend who had moved to Tacoma, Washington. "I fell in love with the Northwest and Seattle," Trish says. "I packed my car and moved up in 1985." She worked at TeleCalc as a test manager. The company used MS-DOS. "I didn't know anything about DOS until I went there." It was there that Trish first heard about Microsoft. She laughs and says, "Microsoft was sort of the Antichrist then. It was called 'the Velvet Sweatshop.' People said they didn't want to work there, but I think secretly they did." When TeleCalc began to go under, Trish struck out on her own as a contractor and eventually took a job at Microsoft as a tester.

Of her interviews at Microsoft, Trish says, "I was thirty-one years old and interviewed by people who were right out of college or five years younger than I was. I knew more about the testing than the testing manager. Some of them were just so arrogant. I never felt so out of place in my life. Some of the questions were typical of Microsoft— very abstract. 'Why is a manhole cover round?' I was a professional contractor coming in to to do a job. But I liked the product, SQL Server, a high-end database engine that lived on a server and processed data quickly. I liked the idea of doing automated testing. It was exciting."

Life at Microsoft

As a software tester, Trish wrote automated test scripts to test the SQL Server engine. They were programs that ran on their own and logged the test results. "I had to learn a new operating system, OS/2. It was close enough to UNIX that I could adapt." Banks, airlines, and companies that do a large amount of transactions use the SQL Server. Sybase owned it and Microsoft licensed it to run OS/2. Trish says, "IBM and Microsoft were still on good terms with their joint project, OS/2. It ran on LAN Manager, which was Microsoft's network software. I had to learn that and the protocols, all the APIs [application program interfaces], and have the workstation talk to the server through LAN Manager. It was a great group. Almost everyone was over thirty except Bob Muglia, who is now a senior VP at the company. I hated Bob in the beginning. He would get right in your face. He was just so passionate about the product."

However, Trish changed her initial impression of Bob when they worked together trying to find a bug in the program. "I was chasing a bug that would appear every once in a while in a random selection of tests. It made the server crash and I could not find it! It was really frustrating. Bob and I did an all-nighter. It was just too funny. I had two server scripts going. We had our feet up on the table and we just watched it. We got to talking and I thought, 'This guy's really cool!' He was incredibly smart, and so passionate about everything he did. We ended up being the best of friends."

In 1990, Trish was hired as full-time employee at Microsoft. She was a program manager for the administrative interface and the API for Visual BASIC for SQL. The company was moving from a character-based interface to an object-oriented interface. "Windows was new and we were all trying to learn it and how the objects behaved." One downside was that as a program manager rather than a people manager, she had no control over the staff who were developing it. She explains. "You do all the design and all the scheduling. You have the ultimate responsibility and none of the power. But I had a great time there even though the group was small."

At Microsoft, Trish worked very hard and put in long hours. She says, "All-nighters were not uncommon. I'd get in about 10 A.M. and work until 7 P.M. I'd go home, get my dog and maybe go to rugby practice. I'd take my dog back to work with me and work until about midnight."

Trish managed her stress levels with regular physical exercise. "I got back into basketball and also played soccer. At Microsoft, you meet people with different interests. If they find out you're athletic, they'll ask you to join a team."

Trish stayed with the group for two years until they shipped version 4.2 of SQL Server. She was responsible for three parts: Administrative, Object Manager, and Visual BASIC API. "They were ready to be shipped out on the same day," Trish notes. "We'd been working crazy hours for almost two years, and I decided to only work ten hours a day. My manager asked me, 'Are you still committed?' We'd been working our butts off! We were just starting another product cycle and we needed a break. You can't think anymore."

Trish started the design for the setup on the NT platform and decided it was time to look for another job within the company. "I wasn't getting promoted, and I thought I deserved it. The group dynamics had changed. There were too few people for the amount of work."

Trish found a job as as a content manager at Technet, a subscription CD that came out once a month. The CD was for technical professionals who supported, designed, and developed systems. "It had articles and white papers that would never be found anywhere else," says Trish. "They were based on people's experiences—very valuable stuff. You didn't have access to on-line because it wasn't around then." When Trish joined the group, the CD was a concept. Microsoft already had the Microsoft Developers Network. "But because MDN was for developers, it didn't have much real-world application," Trish says. Technet would.

Trish was responsible for defining the product and obtaining the content. She hired and managed people who would go out and get the content. "My group had to connect with people in the field. We had to manage relationships. We worked with them to provide us material. We'd fly out to those industry warehouses where they take calls for every computing product under the sun. We worked with what the managers would say to customers who wanted to order CDs and how they should represent Microsoft. We were a diverse group, not only in gender and ethnicity, but also in experience. I loved the product and the team."

While managing that group, Trish had her first experience in putting an employee on a performance improvement plan. "I successfully got him got to do it," says Trish. "Now, he's a big old muck-a-muck at Microsoft. I'm quite proud of him. He was just never given a chance. But I was a reluctant mentor. If I'd had my way, I would have said, 'Okay, if you don't want to be here, go find another job.' But I'm glad I was forced to go through that process. We became friends, and I later recommended him for several promotions over the remaining years that I was with Microsoft."

As busy and hardworking as everyone was at Microsoft, Trish still encountered subtle forms of discrimination. "It wasn't just my personal experience," she points out. "I was a mentor for a lot of African-Americans. When I went to Microsoft I was over thirty. If I'd gone there right out of college, I would never had made it past the first year. I came in with confidence, knowing that I could do the job. I wasn't willing to play the game. I was taught that if you worked hard you would be rewarded. That is not true in corporate America. Not only do you have to work hard, you have to talk up and sell yourself. Some people don't even work that hard—they just talk a lot.

"At Microsoft, there was the myth of the 'golden boy.' It was felt that certain people—99.9 percent of them white males—were earmarked early for success and were given all the tools necessary to succeed. They spent time talking about their work when it was their teams who really deserved all the credit." In Trish's opinion, two exceptions were Bob Muglia and Rick Thompson. "They cared about the product and their people. They spent their time working and not talking themselves up."

Trish points out that many companies, especially high-tech companies, don't have a lot of structure. "If you work someplace like SAFECO Corporation, you know that if you do these twelve things, then you will be rewarded. I would rather work in that type of environment. It isn't just Microsoft. A lot of companies are subjective. The review system at Microsoft is very subjective."

Sometimes discrimination would be evident in the types of jobs woman and minorities were given. "I'd write a piece of code or design an interface a particular way and know that if one of my white male counterparts wrote that same piece of code, there'd be no question about it. As a person of color or as a woman you have to prove yourself. White males get treated totally differently. I've seen some of the interview questions. I could tell from the tone and the follow-up questions what was going on. You would not ask those questions of someone who was like you. That's true everywhere—it's not just a Microsoft thing."

Women at Microsoft shared their frustrations with each other. Trish says, "Women are perceived as being soft and not able to lead. Then, heaven forbid if you have a family and you have to make a choice. Women, just by who we are, are the leaders of our families. It doesn't mean we don't care about our jobs—it just means the job isn't everything to us. We used to wonder if the high-tech industry would ever change. You work at such breakneck speed. There's really no time to think about other people. It seems that young, childless, and one could argue, life-less people run the company. They come right out of college and work so hard because they have no other life."

Socializing created a subtle dimension of bias. "People are willing to work with you if they think they can socialize with you outside of the office. It isn't racist or sexist in the worst way, but it does affect who I am in the company and how I do my work. But by the time I got to Microsoft, I just didn't care. Now I'm over forty and I really don't care what people think about me."

Trish's next job at Microsoft was with a hardware group as a program manager working on the Easy Ball, a big yellow mouse for kids ages two to six. Trish's face brightens as she talks about that group. "That was my product. I wrote the software side of it. I left the group before it shipped, but I did all the core work on it." It was the first time Trish had to design software and drivers for hardware that would run on the yet-to-be-constructed operating system that is now Windows 95. The Easy Ball was supposed to run along with an adult mouse. Trish says, "I was trying to make the PC and the operating system work in a way that it was not meant to work. Quite an experience." Trish enjoyed the group. "They were mature people and a pretty diverse group. It had the first sign of structure that I'd seen at the company. People knew what they needed to do to get promoted.

"Unfortunately, I had just joined that group when I came to a revelation. I cared about diversity in the company and I was now in a position to do something about it. I was working with Patty Stonesifer on some projects, and I decided to move and take a job in the diversity group. That was a very hard decision to make. I loved the group I was with and I knew that if I stayed I could get promoted. We were going to work on more products for kids. I could have worked on Barney Actimate."

Trish went to one of her bosses, Rick Thompson, a senior director, and discussed her dilemma with him. "He looked at me and said, 'I want you to do what you think is best for you. But I think you're going to do this stint in the diversity group and then you're going to leave the company. You won't come back.' He knew that before I did. I was several levels below him, but that's the kind of guy he is—he knows everybody in his group. I apologized for being in his group for such a short time. He had fought for me to be in the group. I was there barely a year. I assured him that I was very happy there, but that I had another calling."

With Rick's blessing and her manager's blessing, Trish took the job of senior diversity administrator. "At that point, I cared enough about Microsoft and my people to believe that I was helping to ensure that they would tap into the minority community."

Trish knew the stats: By the year 2005, 40 percent of the U.S. population would be people of color. The population was already 50 percent women. "I wanted Microsoft to pave the way. I know how loyal African-Americans can be. But the idea is, 'If you screw with me today and you decide to come around tomorrow, I'm already someplace else.' Microsoft already had a bad reputation with people of color, and they needed to turn that around."

But as senior diversity administrator, Trish felt she sometimes went about things the wrong way. "I did it the way Trish had to do it," she says. "I was up front. I'd call people on their stuff. In a lot of cases, I didn't do it very diplomatically. By the time I learned that lesson, I was really frustrated. I don't know any other way to be—that's the problem. In all these years, I never learned to play the game. In the end, in some ways, it became a disservice to me and to the people I was trying to help."

Still, Trish had several key achievements as senior diversity administrator. She was able to get departments to sign up for diversity training. The high school internship program became more of a technical program. Trish was able to convince the recruiting team to think about diversity matters and how they related to other people. "Recruiting was almost all white. They might have two people of color, and we were sponsoring entire events that were focused on people of color." There was a Black Engineer of the Year award, The Society for Hispanic Engineers, and the Minority Career Fair at colleges.

"In one session at a recruiting symposium, someone spoke about how difficult it was to be the only white person in a roomful of people of color. They didn't know what to talk about. I said, 'That's it! That's the kind of stuff I want you to discuss and understand. Now, flip that around. Think about somebody who comes to Microsoft and they have to be here every day. You have the experience for fifteen to twenty minutes and you get to go *home.*' " Trish feels proud to have established that kind of dialogue.

Although she was able to make progress within the diversity group, Trish felt that it wasn't enough. "I had people in positions of power who just didn't care. I focused on future employment and building a pipeline. I did that because I really care about kids. Professional people have already made it. I really cared about recruiting high school and college kids. It's really tough for them."

Trish finally concluded that a company couldn't be changed from the inside. "You have to start over," she says. "I had a theory that if you had a critical mass of people of color who had technical skills, then companies would have no choice but to hire them. Critical mass is crucial. So, I left Microsoft to start over and help that happen."

Life after Microsoft

Trish is the founder of Technology Access Foundation (TAF), whose mission is to bring technology to communities of color. With the financial independence gained from her years at Microsoft, Trish funded the foundation in its first year.

Microsoft has been good to TAF. The company has donated $300,000 in software and given TAF $20,000 in grants. The company has also given TAF easy access to anything they might need. Microsoft employees and retirees teach at TAF, write the curriculum, and do other volunteer work.

At TAF, the William Gates Foundation funds The Virtual Institute. The Virtual Institute is for kids who do not have an interest in computers as a career, but who know they need basic computer knowledge no matter what field they may choose.

TAF's Technical Teen Internship Program is a four-year technical training program for students interested in computers as a career. Students attend two three-hour sessions each week. They must commit to 90 percent attendance and must maintain their grades. The program is in its second year. In the first year, 24 out of 32 students have found internships.

TAF's next focus will be working with children from ages 5 to 12. Trish wants to help them with problem solving and the concept of learning to learn, skills that are not often taught in the schools.

"As a nonprofit, we do one thing differently," Trish says. "I plan a project without caring where the money is going to come from. It's going to come from somewhere. We are talking about kids. There is no waiting. There is a sense of urgency. You can't just sit there and do nothing! We look at TAF as an investment in the future of the United States. Businesses need all levels of technical skills and talents. We need to break the cycle of public assistance and low-paying jobs. TAF offers a solution to both of these issues."

AFTERWORD:

Making It at Microsoft

I proved myself at Microsoft. If you're not good, you're out.

—PAUL SRIBHIBHADH

Microsoft was a kind of high-tech boot camp—either you had what Bill Gates terms "success factors" to make it at Microsoft or you didn't. Clearly, the 12 people profiled in this book had the right stuff. They are a cross representation of Microsoft's first generation of employees who laid the foundation for the company's phenomenal growth and worldwide success. In 1977, when Bob O'Rear joined as employee number seven, the company was a computer-language company. A decade later, the company offered operating systems, several versions of Word and Windows 2.0, entered into a joint venture with IBM to develop OS/2 for the PC, designed a PC version of Excel, created CD-ROM titles, had sold 500,000 mouses, and was making its employees rich thanks to stock options.

Looking back, the prerequisite for success that these 12 had in common was a willingness to take risks. Without acknowledging the sheer guts to take risks, any analysis of their success traits is meaningless. When

Trish Millines moved to San Francisco and later to Seattle without a job, she relied on her own talent, resilience, and abilities to make a fresh start and to succeed. When Ida Cole, Neil Evans, and others left highly successful careers to join Microsoft, a company they knew very little about, they, too, relied on themselves to succeed. Bob O'Rear recalled, "A lot of my friends thought that microcomputers were never going to amount to anything. Mainframes were it. I just didn't know where this company [Microsoft] was headed." The first generation continued to take risks while at the company. In fact, their time at Microsoft was spent stretching their abilities. Neil Evans had to become both a software and hardware person. Scott Oki created Microsoft International from scratch, and Trish Millines left a rewarding job within the company to follow her heart and become its senior diversity administrator.

Once these 12 people arrived at Microsoft, their "success factors" kicked in. Not only were *they* expected to be brilliant and verbally adept, they were expected to create a workplace that demanded those qualities from others. Bob O'Rear expressed it this way: "[When I hired people] I wanted every person to be as smart or smarter than I was. That was the only way the company was going to progress." The process of hiring was extremely important, and at Microsoft, as we have seen, it was done with the same care and commitment that went into each significant technological and business decision. The first generation knew, as Bill Gates and Paul Allen showed by hiring them, how to surround themselves with brilliant and capable people in order to achieve their goals. They set very high standards for themselves and for those they managed. They were confident in their leadership abilities and could inspire others.

The incredible work ethic at Microsoft, the long hours,

working weekends and holidays, is now the stuff of legend. The company is often referred to as "the Velvet Sweatshop." Scott Oki said: "I coined the term 'maniacal work ethic.' I think you have to be a little crazy to work the long hours. But it's all part of the Microsoft culture, and it's not something that feels right to everyone." Some people either can't cut it or refuse to be part of it. Richard Brodie underlined this observation: "I've seen people get chewed up and spit out by Microsoft. It's not for everyone."

For many, success at Microsoft did not translate into a happy personal life. Neil Evans recalled: "My marriage ended, in a large part, because the way I was at Microsoft dominated a large part of my life." In Min Yee's case, "Because of personal problems and work, my health went to hell in a handbasket." Dave Neir echoed others, observing, "It can be hard on the family."

"There's no other place in the world where the expectations are as high and demanding as they are there," said Russell Steele. But, despite the rigors and costs of the physical commitment, those in Microsoft's first generation felt passionate about their work. Microsoft's first generation was a competitive bunch that thrived on confronting challenges and solving difficult problems. Ron Harding said, "People had a very personal commitment to what they were doing. It was a generation of technical people who just loved what they were doing." Neil Evans added to that: "We all felt a kind of ownership in the company, and nobody works harder than the owner."

Once the first generation had set Microsoft's phenomenal growth in motion and established the rules for success, more and more people wanted to work for Microsoft. They wanted to take advantage of the stock options and, if not to stay until retirement, to have Microsoft on their resumes. They understood, as did Paul Sribhibhadh, that if they succeeded at Microsoft, they could make it anywhere. They continued the "maniacal work ethic" and brought fresh energy and enthusiasm to the company. A case in point occurred in the early 1990s. Trish Millines noted, "We'd been working crazy hours for almost two years and I decided to work only ten-hour days. My manager came and asked me, 'Are you still committed?' "

In 1998, Bill Gates, now the richest man in America if not the world, sent this e-mail to his top people. Its subject was the ideal Microsoft employee, who, he wrote, exhibited the following traits:

1. Long-term approach to business, technology, people, customers, and geography; thinks and acts strategically.
2. Results: Gets results, stays focused in driving for results; is relentless in the pursuit of great results.
3. Passion for products and technology.
4. Customer feedback: Builds and uses feedback loops with customers.
5. Individual excellence: Works hard, questions, challenges; learns new things quickly and puts them into action.
6. Teamwork: Works hard to achieve group goals; works efficiently and well with others.

Customer feedback and teamwork are newer concepts within the Microsoft culture. Russell Borland recalled that "up until the late 1980s, there was a strong confrontational style at the company. Microsoft later got infected with the management bug that saw any disagreement as not being a team player." For many "old-timers," this slowed down the company and caused much frustration. The heady, entrepreneurial days were coming to a close. Dave Neir said, "I'm an implementer. I'll get a plan, work on it, and it will get done on time. I left Microsoft because it was getting too big. A staff of 15,000 slows down the wheels of progress." Ida Cole remarked, "The company had grown, and a different approach was needed for its continued success. I was too spoiled to change." Bob O'Rear, who had been at the company the longest, understood the need for change. "The growth of Microsoft has been different every year. It's quite different now. As a company grows larger, you have to have controls." The people who comprised Microsoft's first generation were exactly right for their time. They were the pioneers. Min Yee summed up the early days: "It was all about brains, work speed, and dedication."

The 12 people in this book offer the reader a window into their lives, work, wealth, and ambitions, including their frustrations, challenges, personal sacrifices, and satisfactions. Although each one of them has a unique story to tell, the common elements of their commitment to success would contribute to the development of any business or endeavor. Today, they use their success traits in a myriad of ways, from restoring a landmark theater to creating foundations to forming their own companies. The founders of Microsoft were shrewd to have hired them, for the company's monumental and continuing success would not have been possible without the exceptional work and passion of these key members of the first generation. They held the secrets of business success, and Microsoft's secret was to hire them. Russell Steele said it best. "It's a damn fine company because Bill has surrounded himself with brilliant people. It's okay to have a vision, but if Bill didn't have people to help him carry out and communicate that vision, there would be no Microsoft."

INDEX

Access, 13
  errors in, 64
Accounting systems, xv
African Americans, access to technology,
  229–230, 241
Allen, Paul, xi
  illness of, 18
ALTOS computers, 119
Apple Computer, 135–136, 145
AppleEurope, Multiplan purchase, 38
ASCII, 30, 36
Asian market, 208–210
Association of Thai Software industry, 211
Australia, market potential of, 38–39
Ayala, Orlando, 19

Ballmer, Steve, xiii, 144
  interviewing strategy, 54
  working style of, 100
Banks, Chris, 160, 219, 221
Bartholomew, Craig, 166
BASIC, 74
  arithmetic operations of, 8
  for 8086 chip, 7–8
  macros in, 55
  for RMX80, 9
Bellevue Community College, Center for
  Information Technology in Advanced
  Education, 110
Bettmann Archive, 167
Biker Dreams, 111
Bjerke, Carolyn, 166
Bookshelf, 161, 170, 185
Borland, Russell, xiii, 71–86, 222–223, 246
  background of, 72–74

on Cashmere project, 78–79
on editorial process, 82–83
as manager of Technical Publications,
  77–78
Microsoft press books, 79–82
personal life, 85
post-Microsoft life, 86
retirement, 86
in Technical Publications department,
  75
Word for Windows efforts, 79
workload of, 84
Brainerd, Paul, 45
Bravo project, 53
Bricklin, Dan, 159
Brodie, Richard, xii, 49–68, 245
  Access efforts, 64
  application compiler efforts, 55–56
  background of, 50–53
  code writing strategy, 60–61
  Gates, working relationship with, 65
  as Gates's assistant, 63–64
  learning experience at Microsoft, 65–66
  Microsoft Word development, 56–60
  mouse software support efforts, 59–60
  post-Microsoft life, 67–68
  as programmer, 55–56
  on programming, 61–62
  recruitment to Microsoft, 54
  retirement, 65
  shipping schedules, adhering to, 59,
    60
  and Simonyi, Charles, 52–53
  social development of, 66
  at Xerox PARC, 52–53

Brodie Technology Group, 67–68
Brown, Stephen, 166
Bureaucracy at Microsoft, xvi, 20, 120,
     126–127
  of CBT group, 191
Burr, Raymond, 155
Business structure, development of, xiv
Butler, Jeremy, 123, 142, 202

Cashmere, 63, 78–79
CD-I technology, 170, 184–185
CD-ROM technology, xv–xvi, 152, 157, 161
  business multimedia applications, 170
  content for, 161–162, 164–165
  direction of, 185–186
  pictures and sound on, 187
  special characters on, 187
Children, computer technology training
     for, 229, 241–242
Cinemania, 161
CineWorld, 176
Cole, Ida, xii, xv, xvi, 45, 133–147, 247
  at Apple Computer, 135–136, 145
  background of, 134–137
  on competitive atmosphere, 140–141
  as director of Marketing for Interna-
     tional, 141–144
  Gates, relationship with, 138–140, 142
  health problems, 138–139
  passion of, 145
  post-Microsoft life, 146–147
  on product localization, 142–143
  retirement of, 146
  as vice president of Applications,
     137–141
  on women in business, 144
College of Natural Sciences at the Univer-
     sity of Texas, 21
Combo boxes, 57
Combs, Pat, 166
Compact Disc-Interactive (CD-I), 170,
     184–185
Compaq, 207
Computer-Based Training (CBT) Group,
     190–191
Confrontational style:
  of Gates, 42
  at Microsoft, 42–43, 76, 106–107
Consulting and Professional Services, 135
Continuum, 167
Corbis, 167
Corddry, Tom, 164, 166
Corning, Dave, 123
CP/M, 35
Customer feedback, 246

Databases:
  Access, 13
  Microseed, 13
  SQL, 13
Data General, 95

DENSHO project, 45
Diaz, Gregorio, 19
Digital Equipment Corporation, 93–94,
     96, 101
Digital Research, 11
Diversity at Microsoft, 239–241
Dorling Kindersley, 167–168
Dussault, Dianne Quicker, 177
Dziko, Jill Hull, 229

Easter eggs, 60
Easy Ball, 238–239
8086 chip, simulator for, 7–8
8088 chip, 14
E-mail, at Microsoft, 105
Employee reviews, 103, 139, 189–190,
     237
Encarta, xv–xvi, 152, 161
  interface for, 165–166
  pictures and sound in, 167, 187
Entrepreneurial generation, retirement of,
     xvi
Evans, Neil, xiv, 89–111, 123, 245
  accounting systems design work, 97
  background of, 90–96
  Ballmer, relationship with, 104
  business lessons learned, 107
  contributions to company, 104
  data center design efforts, 101
  on education, 109
  employee review of, 103
  job responsibilities, 100–101
  Microsoft Internal Network development,
     104–106
  OEM business management, 98–99
  packaged products business manage-
     ment, 98–99
  post-Microsoft life, 110–111
  priority setting, 107–108
  retirement of, 108
  stress level, 102–103
  workload of, 102
Excel for Macintosh, 139
Excel '98, 60
Executive Development Institute, 45

Federal Information Processing Standards
     (FIPS), 206
Fiber-optic cable runs, 105
FORTRAN, 7–8
  arithmetic operations of, 8
Frasier, Dave, 128
Freelancers, 192–193
Funk and Wagnall's encyclopedias,
     164–165
Furukawa, Susumu, 37

Gammill, Kevin, 167
Gates, Bill, xi, 159, 225
  confrontational nature, 42
  meetings with, 127–128

Gates, Bill *(Continued)*:
 on microcomputers, 198–199
 personality of, 6
 work ethic of, 11
Gates, John, 152
Gaudette, Frank, 108–109, 123, 126, 144, 146
Getting Past OK (Brodie), 66, 67
Getting Started with Windows 3.1 (Borland), 82
Glaser, Rob, 161
Goldberg, Michael, 29
Gorton, Dee, 155
Government Computer News (GCN), 206–207
Government contracts, 137
Graham, Linda, 19, 39
Graham, Richard, 39
Great Debates, 43
The Great Escape: A Source Book of Delights and Pleasures for the Mind and Body (Yee), 156
Greenberg, Bob, 10
Grove, Andy, 199

Hacking, 51
Harding, Ron, 181–194, 221, 245
 background of, 182–184
 CD-I technology efforts, 184–185
 CD-ROM encyclopedia development, 186–187
 CD-ROM technology efforts, 185–186
 on employee reviews, 189–190
 as hardware-software interface, 192
 managerial style, 189
 on Microsoft work environment, 192
 Omega efforts, 190
 post-Microsoft life, 194
 on Press environment, 188
 retirement of, 193
 software development efforts, 190–191
 sound studio development efforts, 191
 as technical manager of Microsoft Press International, 184–186
 work style of, 188
 on Yee, 188
Hardware improvements, 16
Harris, Jim, 144
Hartman, Alan, 166
Hash tables, 54
Hevron, Richard, 123
Hinsch, Jeff, 222
Hiring policies at Microsoft, xii, 34, 40–42, 94, 145, 244

IBM:
 hardware problems, 14–15
 Microsoft operating system for, 14, 38
 PC definition meetings, 13–14
 PC release, 17
 work environment at, 199

IBM clones, MS-DOS licensing for, 14, 38
IBM Personal Computer Division, 30–31
Information revolution, 110–111
In My Father's House (Yee), 157
Intel:
 culture of, 199–200
 IBM investment in, 199
 microprocessor progress, 16
Intel microprocessor, for 8086 chip, 7
Interactive video systems, 183
Intercontinental Business Division, 19
International market, xiv. *See also* Microsoft International
Introducing Windows 98 (Borland), 85
Ireland:
 offshore manufacturing in, 121
 product localization in, 143
Iwatani, Toru, 159

Jackson, George, 156
Japan, agency relationships with, 36
Japanese-American Chamber of Commerce, 45
Jobs, Steve, 136, 145

Kelly, Ed, 166, 221
Kildall, Gary, 159, 162

Lammers, Susan, 167, 169–170
LAN Manager, 204–205
LAN technology, 200, 204–205
Letwin, Gordon, 101
Lewis, Andrea, 73–75
Licensing, tracking, 97
Lifeboat Associates, 30
Lopez, Tom, 170, 183
 and Yee's multimedia group, 170–171, 185–186
Lotus 1-2-3, 56
Lynch, Peter, 164

Macros, 55
Maniacal work ethic, xii, 40, 245, 246
Manufacturing, offshore, 121
Maritz, Paul, 200, 201
Mason, Chris, 62
Media Vision, 176
The Melancholy History of Soledad Prison (Yee), 156
Memes Central, 67
Merlin, 152. *See also* Encarta
Microcomputers, power of, 12
MicroPro, 28
Microprocessors, 12
Microseed, 13
Microsoft:
 bureaucracy at, xvi, 20, 120, 126–127, 191
 business partners of, 11
 changing markets and, 56
 competitive atmosphere, 140–141

confrontational style at, 42–43, 76, 106–107
culture of, 43, 65, 219, 224–225
database business, 13
designing for the future at, 187–188
discrimination at, 237–238
early products of, 74
and employee personal lives, 245
employee review system, 103, 139, 189–190, 237
evolution of, 243, 247
growth of, 100, 127
hiring policies, 94, 145, 244
ideal employee profile, 246
initial public offering of, 141
Intel products of, 7–8
in marketplace, 193
merit system rewards at, 84–85
multimedia strategy, 161
operating systems business, 35
relocation of, 12–13
reorganization phase, xiii
revenue streams, 30–31, 36
software application design, 29
startup phase of Microsoft, xi
teamwork at, 77
technological capabilities and needs of company, 99
trusting environment, 102, 121
vision statement, 76
work environment, 192–193
work ethic, 9–10, 244–245
Microsoft Australia, 39
Microsoft Development Network, 236
Microsoft Exchange in Business (Borland), 71
Microsoft Information Technology Group, 89
Microsoft Internal Network, 104–106
Microsoft International, xiv, 25
business plan for, 31–32
competition of, 34–35
competition and cooperation within, 121–122
complexity of, 121
culture at, 41, 142
development of, 17
hiring phase, 34
pricing strategies for, 37–38
Microsoft Japan, 37
Microsoft Multimedia Encyclopedia, 152
Microsoft Press, xv, 76, 79–80, 151–152, 158
editorial process at, 82–83
electronic prepress conversion, 220
environment at, 189
innovations at, 225–226
on-line editing, 222–224
profitability of, 160
"Running" titles, 158
success of, 85
titles by, 159, 220–221

Microsoft's International Conference on CD-ROM, 162–163
Microsoft U.S. Domestic Sales Division:
culture of, 40
Great Debates initiative, 43
hiring for, 41–42
Oki as VP of, 39–42
problems of, 39
regard for Microsoft International, 121
Microsoft Word, 38
writing of, 49
Microsoft WordBasic Primer (Borland), 71, 82
Microsoft Word version 1.0:
display speed, 58–59
laser printer support, 57
mail-merge feature, 62
mouse support, 59–60
problems with, 58
spell-check feature, 62
undo function, 61
writing of, 56–59
Millines Dziko, Trish, xi–xii, 229–242, 244
background of, 230–234
on discrimination at Microsoft, 237–238
in diversity group, 239–241
as Easy Ball program manager, 238–239
employee performance improvement plan efforts, 236–237
NT platform design efforts, 236
post-Microsoft life, 241–242
as program manager, 235
as software tester, 234–235
as Technet content manager, 236
work ethic of, 235
Mollman, Peter, 165
Mouse, Word support for, 59–60
MPCs (Multimedia Personal Computers), 164
MS-DOS:
for CD-ROM platform, 162–163
as de facto standard, 97–98
development of, xiii, 3
as international standard, 35–36, 38
Muglia, Bob, 234–235, 237
Multimedia, 152
Multimedia operating systems, 191
Multiplan, 38, 40
version 1.0, 53

Neir, Dave, xiv, xvi, 94, 115–129, 245, 246
background of, 116–118
as Director of International Finance and Accounting, 123–124
international offices setup, 122–123
as manager of central European division, 125
meetings with Gates, 127–128
as Microsoft International controller, 118–119
at Microsoft Press, 125–126

Neir, Dave *(Continued)*:
multiple warehouses plan, 119–120
offshore manufacturing negotiations, 121
post-Microsoft life, 129
retirement of, 126–127
NetWare, 204
Networking technology, 204
Neukom, Bill, 45
Newell, Dan, 167
Nishi, Kay, 36–37
Novell Inc., 204

OEMs (original equipment manufacturers), 17, 18
operating systems for, 35–36
product packaging with computers, 38
records tracking, 97
software licensing, 99, 203–204
Offshore manufacturing, 121
Oki, Scott, xii, xiii–xiv, 25–46, 118, 119, 245
background of, 26–30
children's health and welfare efforts, 44
high-tech investments of, 44
hiring criteria, 41–42
Japanese agency relationships management, 36–37
as Marketing Manager of Special Accounts, 30
MicroPro work, 28, 29
Microsoft Australia development, 38–39
Microsoft International business plan, 31–32
Microsoft International development, 17, 18, 32–33
as Microsoft International vice president, 37
on MS-DOS, as international standard, 35–36
philanthropic efforts, 44–46
post-Microsoft life, 44–46
as senior VP of domestic sales and marketing, 39–42
Sequoia Group development, 27–28
stock options, desire for, 30
work ethic of, 26, 33–34, 43–44
Olivetti, 202–203
Olsen, Ken, 96
Omega, 190
Open standards, 205
Operating systems:
for IBM PC, 14
32-bit, 202
O'Rear, Bob, xi, xii, 3–21, 119, 122, 244, 247
background of, 3–7
BASIC, debates over, 19–20
BASIC and FORTRAN work, 7–9
8086 chip work, 7–8
Gates, impressions of, 11

hardware repair experience, 5
Intercontinental Business Division development, 19
international work, 17
interviewing strategy, 18–19
MS-DOS development work, 14–15
NASA experiences, 5
positions held by, 19
post-Microsoft life, 21
retirement, 20
sales, marketing, and administration work, 17
social life, 10
spy satellite work, 4–5
Ortho Books, 157
OS/2, 204–205
POSIX standard in, 206
for U.S. government, 205–207
Ozzie, Ray, 159

Paramount Theater, 133, 146–147
Patterson, Tim, 14
PC industry, 95–96
P-code, 56
Peterson, Jim, 99
Piracy, 208
Products, localization of, 142–143
Programmers, characteristics of, 61
Programmers at Work, 159
Programming, top-down strategy, 60–61

QDOS (Quick and Dirty OS), 14

Rahal, Jo Ann, 63
Raikes, Jeff, 59, 136–137
Raskin, Jef, 159
Ratliff, C. Wayne, 159
REAL WORLD software, 119
Recruiting at Microsoft, 240
Reed, Mike, 164
Revenue Bomb, 56
RMX80, BASIC for, 9
Roark, Raleigh, 161
Rothschild, Michael, 28
Royalty payments, tracking, 97
Rubenstein, Seymour, 28
Running Microsoft Word for Windows (Borland), 71, 82
Running MS-DOS (Wolverton), 158
Running Outlook 97 (Borland), 85
Running Word 97 (Borland), 85

Sachs, Jonathan, 159
Santa Cruz Operation (SCO), 203–204
Screen dumps, 222
Seattle Computer Products, 14
Sequoia Group, 27–28
Shirley, Jon, xiv–xv, 123–124, 138, 144, 172
Simonyi, Charles, xiii, 52–54, 66, 159
Simpson, David, 19

Singh, Pradeep, 167
Smalltalk, 52
Social life, 10
Social Ventures Partners, 45
Software applications market, 29, 30
Software development, designing for the
    future, 187–188
Software licensing, 99
Source code:
  comments in, 60
  compiling, 56
  Easter eggs in, 60
  sharing, 55
Southeast Asian market, 208–210
Special Delivery Software, 135
Spencer, Phil, 167
Spreadsheets, Multiplan, 38
SQL, 13
SQL Server, 234
Sribhibhadh, Paul, 197–211
  background of, 198–201
  as business development manager for
      Southeast Asian countries, 207–208
  family relationships, 208–209
  as LAN technology manager, 204–205
  as manager of Microsoft Thailand,
      209–210
  networking products dissemination,
      207
  OS/2 promotion, 205–207
  post-Microsoft life, 211
  work ethic of, 207
  as XENIX manager, 201–204
Standard Aero Ltd., 117
Steele, Russell, 215–226, 245, 247
  background of, 216–218
  as composition supervisor at Microsoft
      Press, 219–220
  electronic editing approach, 222–224
  Macintoshes, work with, 220–221
  post-Microsoft life, 226
  Programming Windows work, 222
  work ethic of, 219
Stender, Ray, 155–156
Stock options, xiv, xvi, 95
Stonesifer, Patty, 170, 172–175, 239
Stork, Carl, 122
Success factors, 243–244

Taucher, Mary, 206
Teamwork, 246
Technet, 236
Technical manuals, 81
Technology Access Foundation (TAF), 229,
    241–242
Tempus books, 171
Texametrics, 5
Thailand, market in, 209–211
Thompson, Rick, 237, 239
Time-sharing services, 135
Towne, Jim, 119, 122

Trenary, Jean, 221
Tsang, Rick, 208
Tutorials, sound recordings for, 191
Twips, 57
TymShare, 135

Undo feature, 61
UNIX, 201–202
U.S. government, OS/2 use, 205–207
US West Yellow Pages, 190

Value-added resellers, 204
Vergnes, Bernard, 19, 202
Virtual Institute, 241–242
Virus of the Mind (Brodie), 66, 67
Von Veh, Nils, 166

Wang, 95
Warehouses, 119–120
Warnock, John, 159
Watjen, Craig, 94, 102, 123
Welke, Elton, 76, 126
Wire-wrapped logic, 14–15
Wolverton, Van, 158
Women:
  in business, 144, 238
  for government contracts, 137
Word for the DOS (Borland), 85
Word for Windows, 63, 79
Word for Windows 2.0 (Borland), 82
Word 97 Step by Step Advanced Topics
    (Borland), 85
Word processors:
  Microsoft Word, 56–59
  modes of, 53
Working with Word for Windows (Borland),
    71, 80–82

XENIX, xii, 98, 201–204
Xerox PARC (Palo Alto Research Center),
    52, 53

Yee, Min, xv–xvi, 79, 83–84, 151–177,
    245, 247
  background of, 152–157
  CD-ROM conference initiative, 162–163
  on competitiveness at Microsoft, 171
  on employee qualities, 169
  Encarta design efforts, 165–166
  on Gates, 172
  Gates's trust in, 160
  health problems, 175
  and Lopez's CD-ROM group, 170–171,
      185–186
  management style, 172–175
  movie encyclopedia idea, 171
  multimedia strategy implementation,
      161–164, 167–169
  post-Microsoft life, 176–177
  as publisher of Microsoft Press, 158–159
  quality of books published, 160

AUTHOR'S NOTE:

In the spirit of philanthropy which guides so many Microsoft millionaires, 20 percent of the net profits from the sale of this book will be donated to Social Venture Partners (http://www.svpseattle.org), a charitable foundation. SVP has become a model for meeting the needs of disadvantaged children through contribution of money and the time and expertise of its partners.